Hotshot Trucking

Travel the Country, Make Good Money and Be in More Control of Your Life

Colton Ryder

© Copyright 2019 - All rights reserved.

The content contained within this book may not be reproduced, duplicated or transmitted without direct written permission from the author or the publisher.

Under no circumstances will any blame or legal responsibility be held against the publisher, or author, for any damages, reparation, or monetary loss due to the information contained within this book. Either directly or indirectly.

Legal Notice:

This book is copyright protected. This book is only for personal use. You cannot amend, distribute, sell, use, quote or paraphrase any part, or the content within this book, without the consent of the author or publisher.

Disclaimer Notice:

Please note the information contained within this document is for educational and entertainment purposes only. All effort has been executed to present accurate, up to date, and reliable, complete information. No warranties of any kind are declared or implied. Readers acknowledge that the author is not engaging in the rendering of legal, financial, medical or professional advice. The content within this book has been derived from various sources. Please consult a licensed professional before attempting any techniques outlined in this book.

By reading this document, the reader agrees that under no circumstances is the author responsible for any losses, direct or indirect, which are incurred as a result of the use of information contained within this document, including, but not limited to, — errors, omissions, or inaccuracies.

Table of Contents

Chapter 1- What is Hotshot Trucking?......................7
Chapter 2- Equipment You'll Need In Order to Get Started..18
Chapter 3- Insurance and Other Things You Need To Know to Get Started..44
Chapter 4- How to Get Freight................................65
Chapter 5- What Is Life Like On the Road..............86
Chapter 6- What to Do When the Unexpected Happens on the Road...105
Chapter 7- Common Mistakes Truck Drivers Make That Can Run Them Out of Business....................113
Appendix- Hotshot Trucking Glossary..................123

Introduction

Welcome to the exciting world of hotshot trucking!

In this book, you will learn all about hotshot trucking, how to set up your own business, and how to get loads! From certifications and licenses to the insurance requirements you will be required to carry, this book contains all the information you will need to get started.

I have laid out all of the knowledge on the tools of the trade and all the equipment you are going to require to get started. Including help choosing the right truck and trailer for your business, what equipment you are going to need, and how to maintain everything.

Then, I'll help you understand the certifications, insurance, and licensing you'll need to get on the road, as well as how to use load boards, find freight, and get the best rate per mile.

I've even got you covered once you hit the road with information on how to handle accidents and breakdowns, stay healthy behind the wheel, create a more productive company, be a better driver, and how to avoid many of the common mistakes that owner-operators encounter, especially in the beginning of their hotshot adventure. At the end of this book is an appendix of industry terms you can refer to as you make your way through the book.

I want you to feel confident as you venture into the hotshot trucking business world and this guide will do just that.

Welcome to a whole new world of trucking... hotshot trucking!

Before we get into the nitty gritty of the book please consider leaving a review if you enjoy it. Even just a few words will help other people know if the book is right for them!

Many thanks in advance!

Chapter 1 - What is Hotshot Trucking?

When someone mentions the word "trucking," most of the time, the first thing that comes into people's minds is the classic tractor-trailer 18-wheeler roaring down the open road with multiple trailers being pulled behind it. Massive Class 8 rigs crisscrossing the country and dropping off deliveries to keep the world moving.

Every year, numerous owner-operators start up their companies with the intent of making it big by carving out their own route with their tractor-trailer rig. After investments, fees, insurance, and certifications, many owner-operators find that they can barely make ends meet due to overhead.

Is this the only way? Absolutely not!

Welcome to the world of hotshot trucking!

Hotshot trucking is the use of a Class 3 to 5-truck with various types of trailers to make freight runs. Usually, a truck from one of the big three automakers, this ¾ to 1 ½ ton pickups, are outfitted with trailer connections, either a weight distributing gooseneck or a more common fifth wheel connection, depending on load and trailer type.

The freight comes in all shapes and sizes with most cargo for a single customer and usually under the stipulation that it needs to be delivered as soon as possible. One load may just be across town, while another might take the driver across the country.

From time to time, hotshot trucks are confused with simply being "expedited loads." The fact is that hotshotting is not the load or timing, but the delivery method. Many loads are labeled expedited or time sensitive, but still delivered through traditional methods (Class 8 rigs, delivery, and courier services), and thereby, are not hotshot loads.

A hotshot trucker uses their pickup truck rig and trailers and is constantly on the hunt for their next delivery. Sometimes, they will do numerous loads a day, already looking for their next pickup before they have even dropped off their last one.

Expedited vs. Hotshot

An expedited shipment does not need to be hotshot but a hotshot needs to be expedited. It's like a whale. All blue whales are whales, but not all whales are blue.

In the industry, the term hotshot started getting thrown around as simply meaning expedited. In reality, it only deals with smaller trucks, not the Class Eight rigs. However, there still seems to be some misunderstandings so be prepared to explain this when speaking with people in and out of the trucking industry about what you do.

History of Hotshotting

The 1960s, it was a time of boom in the United States. A time when oil wells began to dot the landscape and industry took hold.

Factories churned out parts to tap the oil fields and couldn't get them out fast enough. Crews constructing those rigs needed parts, but in the wild days of the boom, there were no rush trucking lines or heavy delivery services. And if a rig or equipment broke down, they were losing money every minute while they waited for a replacement part.

Enter the hotshot truckers.

As legend tells it, the term hotshotting originated in Texas in the mid 20th century. A special breed of men started runs from the factories and iron works out to the oil fields. The drivers got drilling and pump parts and equipment out to the locations as quickly as possible, and the boom could continue.

Trucks would line up outside, waiting in the Texas sun for the next part to come out the factory doors. That driver would race the equipment out to the workers at the well or pump. Then, they would turn around and do it all again.

There was a constant flow of parts and the drivers made very good money delivering for the cash-rich oil industry.

However, over the years, the boom began to wane and delivery techniques changed. Companies began to consolidate and created their own fleets to handle deliveries in-house. Drivers needed to turn to other delivery sources and began to actively drive for private parties and other businesses.

Why is Hotshot Trucking So Awesome?

Hotshot trucking can be very fun as well as a chance to make money and be your own boss on your own terms. You still get the thrill of running loads without the crushing regulation, overhead, and some of the safety issues.

Lower Start-Up Costs

You can start your business without purchasing an expensive Class Eight rig, dual axle, or other work truck. Investment in your truck should run under $40,000, which is much smaller than what is required for a big rig. And if you purchase a used truck after checking it out carefully and maintaining it, your vehicle costs could be even lower.

Fuel Costs Are Lower

If you drive a Class 8 tractor-trailer rig with two 150-gallon gas tanks, it can easily take over $1,500 just to fill up. It's one of the major costs and financial issues for 18-wheeler drivers.

However, if you are running a hotshot truck, your fuel costs are going to be far lower. Your tank is most likely going to be in the range of 40 gallons and your miles per gallon is going to be higher than a Class 8 truck. However, you will be hauling freight and the size and weight will affect your truck's MPG, but it will never approach the cost of a semi rig.

Truck Maintenance

Class Eight owner-operators can spend tens of thousands of dollars a year on maintenance of their truck. As a hotshot trucker, if you purchase wisely, your cost should be minimal, especially if you purchase new. For the first few years, you should just have general maintenance costs and many issues that could pop up will be covered under warranty.

Documents and Certifications are Fewer

You'll still have some things you have to do, but it's not what it would take to start up a Class Eight trucking business. Licensing is also much easier. Depending on your state, you may not even need a Commercial Driver's license.

Pay Rate

Without the overhead of an 18-wheel rig or Class 8 rig, you have the ability to make more money. You can often get multiple loads in a day and don't have to worry about giving a cut to the business since you are the business owner.

You truly have the potential to make as much money as you would like. There are some hotshot drivers who only do it part time and add $10 to $20 thousand to their pocket every year. However, most drivers work full time and if they are careful, attentive, and very hard working, they can clear $200,000 annually.

As a hotshotter, you also shouldn't have to deal with a large number of terminals, hubs, or loading docks where a Class Eight driver sometimes has to wait hours to clear their load or pick up a new one. Often, your customers will be average people who just need things moved or you'll be dealing with smaller companies. Also, since your loads are being rushed, usually they will be ready for pick up when you arrive.

Variety

Hotshot trucking can actually be fun because you never know what your next load might be. The thrill of discovery definitely plays a role in the excitement of the job.

Something that is important about a career is that it is something you enjoy. And the constant change of freights, even within the same overall category is fun and keeps you on your toes as an owner-operator.

You'll need to put your logic skills to the test figuring out how to load some freights and secure them as well as maneuvering certain access roads and locations. It's definitely a job that makes you think and that, in itself, can be fun.

And if you are a people person, this is the job for you. You'll get to meet new customers and clients as you work with them. Even if you are more of an introvert, this job is still great for you. You can get a load and get on your way to the solitude of the road.

You Can Sleep At Home If You Want...

You don't have to do long hauls across the country if you don't want to. While it ultimately depends on your area and specialty, if you stay local or regional, you can be home to sleep in your own bed.

If you live near an industrial area, oil fields, or other construction heavy regions, you can schedule several hauls for the day and have dinner with your family.

Or You Can Travel!

Hotshotting gives you a chance to travel on your own schedule. Depending on available jobs, you can schedule trips and have them pay for themselves. You'll also be able to make more for traveling because you get paid by the mile.

Flexibility

As the owner–operator of your own hotshot trucking business, you have flexibility in what, when, and where you want to carry. You can set your own hours, as few or as many (legally) that you want to drive.

Opportunity

With the boom of online businesses, the rules and demands have changed. There are more and more shipments being sent out that require Class 8 deliveries leaving more and more jobs for smaller freight being left without drivers.

It's estimated that there is a shortfall of about 50,000 drivers in the United States. So when it comes to your business and looking for jobs, they are out there just waiting for you.

People will always have things, and those things will always need to be transported. So whether it's moving a specially designed drilling part to the next state or moving a cherished backyard playhouse to someone's new home, there are always going to be jobs.

Freedom

You have the freedom of a driver and a business owner. Nobody knows how to run your business better than you. As you gain more experience, you become better at running your business.

You can develop it in any way you want. For example, there are a number of hotshotters who specialize in moving classic and exotic cars and do quite well, others in medical supplies. The important part of freedom is to have a plan but stay flexible as you develop your business.

Even if you want to take the day off, you can. However, you may find that you don't want to take many days off because you are thoroughly enjoying what you do and also like the money you make.

Openings for Women Drivers

Over the years, a stereotype has grown that in order to be a successful truck driver, the driver must be a man. This could not be further from the truth.

Hotshot trucking is an amazing opportunity for women drivers. Currently, the entire trucking industry is seeing a huge deficit of drivers. Remember that study that said 50,000 more drivers are needed to meet the freight shipping demand? And there is no reason female drivers can't help fill the gap.

Hotshot trucking is also an amazingly level playfield for drivers of either sex. When you bid for a load on the load board, all they care about is your rate and history. They don't even need to know who is driving if it's just your company profile. So, this creates a powerful opportunity for equal pay.

However, there are still challenges such as sexual harassment. Unfortunately, it does still happen from other drivers and clients. And unfortunately, since as a hotshot driver you aren't dealing with an overarching business or corporate control, it is something that will need to be handled by legal matters if necessary.

Safety can be an issue for women drivers, as it also is for male drivers. Alone on the road and in uncertain situations, all drivers need to always be aware and careful.

Yet, other things have changed. In the old days, equipment was heavy and unwieldy, often having to be operated manually by someone large and strong. While some equipment may still be bulky, much of it is now technologically advanced. In many occurrences, the heavy winch handle has been replaced by a button or switch.

The bottom line is that hotshot trucking offers a great opportunity for making money and growing your business and it doesn't matter if you are a man or a woman as long as you are willing to put in the hard work.

What if I'm completely new to trucking in general?

You might be reading this and concerned that since you haven't been a trucker or in the business, you can't do this. That is absolutely not true.

There is going to be a learning curve, but that is true with any business. You'll make mistakes quickly, and you'll learn the best and most efficient way to operate your hotshotting business.

There are some steps that you can take to help with the curve.

- Do your homework. Research everything you can online and stay current with newsletters, websites, and podcasts. There is an entire hotshotting community out there and you can learn from their experience and maybe avoid a few missteps along the way.
- Learning the vocabulary of trucking is going to help you greatly. While hotshotting is its own world, there

is a great deal of carryover in language and in terminology. Names for truck parts, slang for actions, and even some of the CB language are definitely in use. I have included some for you in the appendix at the end of the book.
- Try to be positive. Life and business can get rough. There may be dry spells on the way to profitability, but remember that hard work pays off.
- When you need it, ask for help. Ask hotshotters or truckers with experience or maybe consider taking a class from a trucking school. They offer classes in hotshotting and can provide a great base of information.

Chapter 2 - Equipment You'll Need In Order to Get Started

There are definitely some basic things you need to get started in hotshot trucking- such as a truck and trailer, but you will find there are other necessary items as well and some that can not only make your business easier but safer and more profitable.

With all of your equipment from the largest truck down to the smallest strap, make sure you inspect for any wear or tear that might lead to breakage. If possible, always get a manufacturer or sellers guarantee on paper to take care of any future issues.

Don't be afraid to compare the shops either. Of course, saving thousands on a large item like a truck or trailer is a big help. You'll find, as a business owner, that smaller savings on items add up and will help you stretch your small business dollar further.

You are going to find very quickly that a great number of the decisions you need to make are going to be based upon the type of freight you will be hauling. Spend some time on this question and do your homework. Look into the types of loads that are available on load boards. (More on load boards to come). What types of loads are paying well? How many are in your region? Are there specialty loads you see a lot of?

You'll also need to have your preliminary numbers worked out. Ask yourself the hard questions about how much the business can afford or finance for a truck and trailer. If you are starting an LLC, are you going to pay through it? Once you have these general numbers and a plan, you'll have a better idea of where to start in your vehicle, trailer, and equipment search.

If you don't have a specific type, then keep your options open and give yourself the most amount of leeway as possible. If you aren't going to be specifically hauling things that need a covered trailer, then don't get one. Have you come to the conclusion you'll only be hauling items at the lower end of the weight range? You might want to consider a smaller truck or pass on the diesel or duallies.

As a small business owner and a driver-operator, there are going to be a lot of decisions you'll need to make before you even take your truck for a test drive.

Truck

There are nine classes of trucks ranging from the light truck all the way up to the Class 9 super size truck. While the well-known 18-wheeler is a Class 8, you'll be concentrating on Class 3, 4, and 5 trucks. There is a breakdown of all classes listed in the appendix at the end of the book.

Cost

As you plan out your company, one of your first big decisions is going to be whether you should buy a new truck or a used one. The price you are going to pay is obviously going to depend on what make, model, and extras you get on your truck.

In purchasing a new one, you know everything works and is under warranty if anything goes wrong. But with a new hotshot truck in the range of $35,000 to $70,000 depending on what you get, it might be too much to make the bottom line work.

If you buy a used truck, you are going to save a lot of money and you might be able to get a limited warranty, but they usually don't cover very much and you'll end up paying out of pocket in repairs over time.

When you reach a point where you are spending more on repairing your truck than you would on the payments on a new one, it is probably time to consider trading up.

If you do purchase a used truck, make sure you get it checked out by a qualified mechanic before agreeing to purchase.

Type of Truck

There is as much advice out there on the right truck to use as there are trucks out there. Drivers (hotshot and otherwise) will argue till they are blue in the face about how this brand of truck is better than that one, etc. It really comes down to two things: personal choice and the bare statistics of the vehicle. Well that, and price of course.

Size and Style

The first decision is what size of truck to purchase. Think about what type of freight you will be hauling and what type of trailer you will be using. Do you need something at the top of the hauling range or are you going to be dealing with smaller types of loads?

Investigate the hauling capacity of different trucks as well as their reviews and recall history. Ask yourself if you want to purchase a truck that is large enough for your business right now or a situation where you will be growing into it.

You may decide that you should get the largest capacity truck like or you may find that something smaller can work. However, look into repair costs. A smaller truck may take on more wear and tear dealing with a large trailer and while repairs may be less expensive, they can be much more frequent. If you go with a larger truck, it may handle loads better and have fewer repairs, but when you do, they may be very costly.

Next question, is a new truck or a used one right for you? Again, check reviews and history of truck brands and styles. Also, look into fuel mileage and repair histories of similar models.

Personal taste also factors into the purchase. While you shouldn't spend a great deal more money just because of a nameplate if all other things are the same, you will be spending a lot of time behind the wheel and you should like your truck. Make sure it is comfortable for you. Some trucks are not made for taller drivers and if you're tall, this can create issues on long hauls or just daily driving. Make sure the style of truck allows you not only to be able to see all your controls but reach them unhindered.

Check It Out

If it's new, you have an easier time checking the history of a vehicle, because it has none. If it's fresh off the lot with only dealer miles, you don't need to bring it to your mechanic (or bring them with you) to check out how it has been taken care of. You can always bring a mechanic friend with you and they can explain any potential issues or certain features on the truck. That never hurts.

If you are purchasing used, do your homework. Look up records on the model you are contemplating. Many used car dealers will offer free Car Fax information so you can see the history of the vehicle. If they don't, it may be worth it to run your own check. It will list any accidents as well as the maintenance history of the truck.

Also, run a check for recalls or safety issues with the model you are checking out. And definitely have your mechanic check out the vehicle for any issues, proper maintenance, or signs of misuse.

To Finance or Not To Finance?

If you are purchasing a new truck, most likely, you cannot afford to pay for it in full with cash. Even if you can, it's probably not the best idea for a business just starting out.

Your capital- or the cash you have to begin your business with- is going to be needed for a number of things. You may even have times when you aren't pulling in the loads you want or need to pay your bills, so you will need to dip into your cash reserves. By financing, you will have more of your cash in emergencies and to help grow your business.

Do your research on dealers before you shop. Look for reviews from customers about their experiences and vehicle purchases. Never make snap decisions and always be willing to walk away, either to look at another lot or to give serious thoughts to your potential choice.

If you are buying a used truck, in this day and age, most dealers have payment plans or financing options. You may want to consider shopping at one of the new generation car dealers. There is no haggling, each vehicle is checked and guaranteed.

Another way certain companies do business that could benefit you is that you can get approved for financing with them before you begin shopping. Then, you know exactly what you can afford, what your payments are going to be, and the search is made easier.

Another aspect of a generational car dealer is that their entire national inventory is online, so you can shop from your local location or one across the country. If you decide on a certain truck, you can pay a small fee and they will transport it to you quickly and safely.

Also, check with your bank or credit union about vehicle financing to see what sort of rates you can get versus those offered by dealers.

Dual Tires?

A dually truck has an extra set of tires in the rear, hence the dually name. When you are shopping for your truck, you may have the option in the model you are considering.

Duallies offer an increase in maximum towing payload capabilities. It also can be much more stable for a trailer.

It does, however, lead to a decrease in the fuel economy and is a great deal more expensive than the traditional four-tire style. It also can make for more difficult parking and loading because of its increased width. Plus, when it comes time to get new tires, you have to pay extra for a larger number of them.

Gooseneck vs. Trailer Hitch

There are two types of trailer hitches for you to consider in your decision. This will obviously play into your choice of trailer you purchase as well.

A gooseneck trailer hitch is a large metal hitch that connects in the bed of your truck. The other type is a fifth wheel hitch, otherwise known as a bumper hitch or trailer hitch. Fifth wheel hitches are much more common since they are versatile and used on a larger number of trailers, both commercial and recreational. Gooseneck trailer hitches are usually seen in industrial trailers that need to be sturdier or carry more load weight.

Fifth Wheel
- Generally gives you a smoother ride
- Wider turn radius

- Less expensive
- Easier to park and store
- Better for novice drivers

Gooseneck
- Offers more stability
- Has a tighter turn radius
- Trailer sway is limited
- Heavier
- Extra installation cost and time of hitch
- Being an experienced driver helps in use

Gasoline vs. Diesel?

Ah, the age-old truck debate... gasoline vs. diesel. There are pros and cons to both sides. The truth is you might not even have to make the choice, but if it does come up, here's what you need to know:

- Diesel engines offer a 30 to 35 percent increase in fuel economy when compared to gasoline engines. The reason is that the diesel engine production process burns less fuel than a conventional engine.
- If you are buying new, the option of a diesel engine on Class 3 or 4 trucks can be between $5,000 and $8,000.
- Gasoline is more readily available at retail stations.
- Diesel is more expensive than gasoline.
- Diesel maintenance and repair costs tend to be higher.
- Diesel engines last significantly longer than gasoline engines. Its construction restyle requires sturdier parts. Also, the exhaust given off by diesel is not as corrosive as gasoline, so the diesel engine will last longer.
- Diesel does give you a torque advantage when towing. Diesel fuel ignition allows the engine to deliver power at a lower RPM.

- Diesel trucks usually have better resell ability than a comparable gasoline truck. Because they tend to have more life in their engine, their value stays higher.

So which one? Well, as I said, each has its pros and cons. But in reality, it will probably come down to what you can afford and what is available. If you are shopping new or used and want a diesel, it doesn't' mean you are going to find one in your price range and with the setup you want. You may have to make a decision based simply on what is available to you.

Sound System

It sounds silly at first but think about it. You are going to be spending hours in the cab of your truck and are going to be listening to something. Whether it's talk radio or music, you'll want to be able to hear and enjoy it.

So, as you look into new trucks, make sure to check out sound systems and upgrades. It might be better to go with an aftermarket upgrade, depending on your needs and wants.

If buying a used truck, make sure to check the sound system out for shorts or blown speakers. If the system has problems, upgrade it with an aftermarket installation based upon what you listen to.

Your needs are really going to depend on what you listen to and how it is delivered. Later in the book, I'll discuss the different types of entertainment often favored by drivers.

Color, Wraps, and More

Yes... color. It may seem frivolous, but the color of your truck can be important.

If you are branding your company, choosing the color of the truck can actually be a way to build that brand. Depending on how you want to promote and present your business, you may want to consider wraps. These will cover larger parts of your truck and potentially your trailer. Or you can wrap the entire thing.

Also, consider how certain colors may show dirt or light damage that trucks or trailers can unfortunately sustain.

You can have your logo and contact information displayed. A wrap job will run several thousand dollars minimum, not including any design work. However, it could be a good investment when it comes to advertising.

One word of advice is to not paint your truck yourself unless you are a professional painter. You don't want a truck that looks like it was done over unprofessionally because it will reflect on your own abilities as a driver-owner. Keep your truck presentable and professional-looking, as well as clean and kept up. Often, your truck will be your calling card and you want people to have the best first impression possible.

Trailer

After finding your hotshot truck, getting the right trailer is a close second in importance.

Begin by asking yourself three questions: what types of freight do you plan to carry, how much will it weigh, and how large is your budget?

Types of Trailers

There is a multitude of trailers available for different jobs; you will most likely only have one or two that can be used for hauling various types of freight.

To begin, do you want a closed trailer or an open one? Each has its pros and cons and really comes down to the type of freight you will be hauling. If it is smaller and valuable, then you might want to consider a closed trailer that you can protect freight from the elements and lock it in from potential thieves. While you can get a closed trailer as large as something that can carry a car, it will limit you in your load's width and height.

Consider the construction of the trailer and what it is made of. Again, it comes down to the type of loads you see yourself hauling. Do you need something with framing or a rack? Does it need to be covered and lockable? Or is a simple flatbed truck going to suffice?

Look into the construction of the trailer and make sure it's road and freight-worthy. Make sure it's not just welded together and that it is intended to undergo the rigors of highway-freight hauling.

Trailer Length

To begin, remember that the longer your trailer, the heavier it is going to be. There's more to it, so it's going to weigh more. And you have a maximum weight limit, so that added length is going to take away from that.

A shorter trailer will limit some of your cargo options, but it will be more maneuverable and give you higher speed abilities. You are most likely going to settle on something in the range of 20 to 40 feet.

Based upon the type of cargo and the type of truck you have, look into different coupling options. It might be better to install a gooseneck coupler in the bed of your truck or use the standard hitch coupler with some additions. This will not only affect the types of load you carry but how you drive your truck because based on where the coupling is, it can affect the handling and turning.

Appearance is not only important from a professional standpoint but for safety. Check the paint job for rush spots or bad welds. Look over the wiring and make sure it is not faulty and adheres to any DOT rules and regulations. Make sure you have the necessary taillights and or reflective points.

Buying Used

If you decide to purchase a used trailer, there's absolutely nothing wrong with that choice, as long as you do your homework and make sure there aren't any surprises. It's really not much different than buying used cars, except there are fewer things to check.

Make sure to use this checklist as you examine your potential new-used trailer:

- Look at the trailer as a whole and pay close attention to the design. Just because it's in good shape and maybe flashy, it doesn't mean it's going to work for you and your truck. Examine the design, weight limit, and make sure it'll work for your needs.
- Check the frame closely for wear, cracks, breaks, or other wear and tear or damage. Some may be fixable while others may be a sign of more trouble down the road.
- Examine the wheels and tires. You may need to replace them due to age or use. Look for cracking. Take a look at the ground. Is the grass growing up around the tires? It means it's been there a while; the tires may be unusable.
- Also, make sure they are the proper tires in size and style for a trailer. However, look closer at how they have worn. Uneven tread wear could be a sign of an uneven or bent axle.
- Take a close look at the brakes, brake drum, rotors, and shoes. Also, take a close look at the wiring. Bring a voltage meter or other device to check for shorts and proper connections.
- Inspect the floorboards or deck of the trailer. If wooden, look for rot or breakage. If metal, examine for rust, bending, or other damage.
- Make sure that you take a very close look at the coupler. Is it clean, rust-free, and unbent? Is it the

proper coupler for not only your truck but for the types of loads you plan to carry? If not, take into consideration how much it will cost to replace.

Aluminum or Steel?

There are many decisions for you to consider when purchasing your trailer and another is what it's made of. In choosing between aluminum and steel, there are a few factors to contemplate.

When it comes to cost, a steel trailer is usually less expensive, but maintenance costs tend to be higher than aluminum. With steel, you will need to be concerned with anticorrosion measures, paint, and integrity issues. If you work in a location in close proximity to salt water, this will increase the rust on your trailer, which could lead to a breakdown in its integrity.

Aluminum trailers are lighter, so you'll have more room below your maximum for cargo. Usually, they are about 15% lighter than steel, so that means you can carry 15 percent more freight and that can make you more money.

Steel and aluminum trailers both have about the same strength factor, but aluminum will bend without breaking. Steel is more rigid, which can be important depending on your load.

Aluminum trailers also tend to last longer, the main culprit being the rust factor.

In the end, the choice is up to you, it comes down to what you need and what you can afford. Aluminum has a small edge due to the cost factor after the initial outlay. However, if you are just starting out, you might just need to get the best trailer you can for the amount of money you have budgeted.

Air Ride Suspension: Is it worth it?

Available on newer trailers or added for an extra cost, air ride suspension uses woven rubber and polyurethane air-spring bags to give you a smoother ride. It also gives you the ability to raise and lower the height of your trailer.

Using air ride suspension can offer a better fuel economy because you can lower your trailer height and get less wind resistance on a smooth road. You can also change the height on different terrains so your trailer performs as well as possible.

Air ride suspension is also great for fragile roads because the system will keep the trailer even and all wheels on the road. It will assist the trailer from rolling on corners and freight being damaged. It also reduces the wear and tear on your trailer due to less vibration, bouncing, and jarring.

However, there are some issues that you will encounter with the air ride system. It requires much more maintenance and is very expensive to install. Also, as a driver, you need to learn exactly how the system works and how and when to alter the settings.

As an owner-operator, you will need to decide if the price is worth it to your bottom line. It might be something to wait until your business takes off and you upgrade your trailer. It also depends on what type of freight you will usually be hauling and the types of roads you will be traveling over.

Specialty Trailers

After a time, you may discover that you are starting to get a lot of loads in one specific area. It might be agriculture, medical, or even produce or perishable items. At that point, you might want to consider modifying your trailer or purchasing an additional one. Later on, we will be talking about developing niche contracts.

It really depends on how you approach your loads and who your clients are. You may find it's worthwhile having a second trailer that is enclosed, even though you only use it a few times a month. However, those jobs easily pay for it and make it worthwhile to have. It all comes down to economics.

You can look into renting trailers for special jobs for one-time delivery or a series of them. Be careful about purchasing a trailer with the intent of finding the work it's right for. Only purchase a second trailer (or specialty) if you have a plan and know that it is going to go into use and not just sit in the backyard, rusting away.

Equipment

There is a gear that you will need for your loads. Some of the items are general things that you will use constantly, but there will be specifics you'll find you'll need based upon the load. As you start to make more and more deliveries, you'll find your specific uses for certain items and may even rig up some of your own. You'll probably find the best way to tie down crates and maybe even change a strap fitting so it works specifically for that load. That's part of the fun of hotshotting!

Constantly check the state of your equipment, especially your straps. Look for wear, cuts, and tears.

Some gear lasts a lifetime like tools and some straps, so always be on the lookout for them at auctions or even garage sales. You never know what you may find.

Gearbox

Your first consideration will be some type of gear or equipment box (or chest) to store your equipment. You may be tempted to just dump it all in the bed of your truck but this is a bad idea for several reasons.

First of all, your gear will get dirty, damaged, or stolen in the bed of the truck. Even coiled or wrapped up ropes, chains, and straps can become tangled and fouled by rolling around the bed of the truck. If you have a gooseneck hitch, you run the risk of something hitting or becoming tangled around the workings. You may even find that your equipment flies out on an especially bumpy road and you'll arrive at your pickup spot without the ability to secure your load. Not to mention you'll be leaving them exposed to the elements and lessening their lifespan significantly.

With a gearbox, you can lock up all your equipment and keep it organized and safe. You'll always know where it is and be able to concentrate on your jobs. It is a moment where the organization can truly save you time, trouble, and money.

You have two options for your gearbox, depending on your truck and trailer setup. First, you can get a box for the bed of your truck. There are several styles, but make sure it doesn't interfere with any hitches and that it is always accessible. Also, make sure you can lock it and you have spare keys.

A second option is a trailer box. Some drivers will add a specially designed gearbox to their trailer near the front or header board. If you decide to do this, take special care that the gearbox does not interfere with your towing or its position. Also make sure that the weight does not affect your driving or handling of the trailer. The gearbox might need to be built from scratch. Some truckers will simply make the box an extension of the metal frame, or you'll need to retrofit a gearbox to fit and connect to your trailer. This is about the time you realize as an owner-operator that you want to make friends with a welder if you don't already know how to do it yourself. It's a skill that can really help you with many tasks and maintenance.

Straps, Lines, and the Chains

Every load is unique and you will quickly learn when and how to use straps, ropes, and chains. Make sure that you have a wide selection of straps, ropes, and chains for every occasion.

Also, make sure you maintain them and put them away in an orderly and proper fashion. Wrap up straps and keep the buckle clean and well-oiled when needed. Also, check for rust. Keep ropes properly wrapped up as well as chains. Make sure they are clean and tangle-free.

Tarps

Keep a selection of waterproof tarps in your truck or gearbox. These are very helpful for protection against the elements and to help keep prying eyes from seeing what's on your trailer.

Always make sure to dry off any water or clean away any dirt or other substances on the tarps and fold them properly before putting them away.

Ramps

Depending on what types of freight you haul, you may need ramps to roll up onto your trailer. Keep them in good working order and check for metal shards or anything that could damage tires as vehicles are loaded onto the trailer. Check the weight rating and make sure to not overweigh the ramps. In a pinch, you can use wooden runners of lumber, but it is highly recommended you get some rated metal ones. Ramps are also useful for moving things on to the trailer using hand trucks, carts, or forklifts. Usually, they can be attached or rolled up into the trailer. However, if they are aftermarket, you may need to create some sort of storage system for them.

Locks

Keep a series of locks in your equipment box. Make sure you have the keys on yourself at all times. Don't use combination locks because the combinations can be easily forgotten and many cheap combo locks can be broken with a simple hammer.

Bolt Cutters

These can come in very handy to cut chains and locks if keys are lost, or if combinations are forgotten.

Pallets

Pallets are wooden or plastic platforms that freight is often attached to for shipment. Their construction is such so that you can attach freight to the boards as well as strap them down to a trailer or easily lift them with a forklift.

They are usually very plentiful and can be used until cracked and nearly falling apart. You should replace them when they reach this point because they may damage the freight when lifted by a forklift.

Even though plentiful, it would be handy to keep some of these in better condition on hand. You may even want to keep a few strapped to your trailer or truck in case they are needed.

Communication

In the old days, it was only the CB radio that truck drivers had to communicate with home and each other. Or the quarter-driven pay phone at the truck stop.

Now, with the proliferation of cellular and smartphones, communication has never been easier. However, not all plans are the same so do your research.

Compare the shops to find the plan that is right for your business. Pay attention to not only the cost but the data limits and roaming fees, especially if you are traveling out of state.

There are also a number of smartphone apps out there that can help you with your trucking business. From GPS and locations to load board apps and invoicing. Many of these apps are free initially but may require further purchases for the full usefulness. Make sure to add these costs to your business budget.

Clothing and Footwear

You will need proper clothing while loading and driving. A lot of your wardrobe will be based upon your climate. You probably don't want to wear shorts if you are hotshotting in Alaska in the winter, but it's really up to you.

Often, the best advice is to dress in layers because you may find weather changing rapidly as you drive and it's much easier to take away layers than it is to add layers that you don't have with you.

Also, bring extra clothing to change into after long drives or because you may rip or dirty what you are wearing. There's nothing worse than being caught hauling in a rainstorm and not having dry socks and underwear to change into.

Also, find solid comfortable work boots (steel-toed is suggested for loading and unloading cargo, but they might be too much for driving). You will find that you need at least one pair of tough work gloves as well. Make sure to invest in quality, thick gloves.

When traveling overnight, don't forget your change of clothes, sleepwear, and toiletries.

Safety equipment

You will need (and in some areas be required) to have safety equipment in your truck. Make sure you have a reflective vest, hard hat (some locations to haul to may require you to wear this while on site), road flares and triangles, and other safety gear.

Hard Hat

Many worksites will require you to wear a hard hat on the property, so you might as well get your own instead of sharing the community helmet. Plus, you can always personalize it.

Rain gear

Find room for a rain poncho, pants, and headwear. There will be times where you will need to load or unload your freight in the rain and you'll be thankful you have this. Not to mention, if you are ever broken down, dealing with a tire or a loose strap in a downpour, you'll be thrilled you have this protective clothing.

A handy item to have is a rain bag that you can put muddy clothes into until you can clean them. Always remember to remove it from the truck and wash them as soon as you can.

Tool Kit

While major breakdowns and mechanical issues will usually require a visit to a mechanic, often you'll be able to handle smaller issues on the road. We will go further into this in a later chapter, but make sure you have a basic tool kit with you in the truck. Include basic tools like a hammer, wrenches, screwdrivers, a drill, and drill bits.

Keep them in a small lockable toolbox. A suggestion is to figure out where the best place in your truck or cab is to keep a case, take measurements, and get the proper size toolbox. You can always keep it in your gearbox as well.

If you are keeping your toolbox in the cab of the truck, consider using Velcro to attach it in place. This method works well and can be used for many items from a medical kit to your phone.

Emergency Kit

Your emergency kit is different from your safety kit; however, in times of distress, you may find yourself using both.

While not limited to it, the largest item in your emergency kit is probably your first aid kit which should include bandages, pain relievers, gauze, rubbing alcohol, and wet wipes. Some truckers will also include an emergency credit card or cash as well as a supply of water, a knife, spare clothes, and emergency bars for nutrition.

Cleaning Kit for Truck

Your truck is your tool and a true craftsman cares for his tools. This also means keeping it clean. Not only is this for presentation, but it helps with a professional attitude on the road.

Keep soap, sponges, brushes, and other cleaning supplies in your truck. Truck and car self-wash facilities are easy to find and it doesn't take long to spruce up your rig.

Also, keep the inside clean. Throw away old papers, food, and wrappers. Wipe down your dashboard regularly to remove dust and debris.

There are always services that will wash your truck at an assortment of locations or even come to you. However, these are expenses that can be easily saved if you do the cleaning yourself. Plus, there is a bit of pride to the feeling of polishing up your own rig.

You'll find that you may even feel more active and vital in a clean cab.

Always remember that your truck and trailer are a symbol of your business and professionalism. You may not lose the job when you pull up in a dirty, unkempt truck and rig, but when the client shares their experience, you know that'll be something they talk about. Always put your best foot forward.

Maintenance

It is imperative that you maintain your truck, trailer, and equipment. They are your lifeblood, and without them, your business will go under immediately.

Create a checklist to go over before you leave on any run. Depending on your rig setup, it may be short or long, but make sure it is complete.

As for regular and more in-depth maintenance, there are some things you can handle while others will require bringing your truck or trailer into a mechanic. Always use a reputable mechanic or service shop.

Truck

- Follow a regular tune-up, oil change, and tire rotation schedule.
- Immediately have any service lights checked. Consider getting your own alert checker to see if it's something serious.
- Consider installing a vinyl or plastic bed liner. This can protect from wear, tear, and rust.
- Always check the underside of your truck, especially if you have driven in an area with snow and where road salt is used. You might want to consider rust prevention coating or other measures.
- Make sure all belts are regularly inspected and replaced when necessary.
- Keep detailed maintenance logs for your truck (and trailer).
- Read and understand your owner's manual. Not only will you understand your vehicle better, but you may also learn things that save you money like small maintenance or repairs you can do yourself. You may be able to save a great deal of money by learning to change your own oil, spark plugs, or filters.
- Regularly check your own fluids such as antifreeze, power steering fluid, coolant, oil, and wiper fluid.
- Check the truck battery regularly for leakage and that the connections are tight.
- Replace your windshield wipers regularly. Know that if you live in an area with heavy weather, they will need to be changed more often.

Trailer

- Keep it clean, but also dry, especially if it's a steel trailer. Overexposure to any moisture, even washing can lead to rust.
- Make sure the floor system is proper for your cargo. Also, check it regularly to make sure there are no cracks in the wood or metal.
- Take in for service for brakes and wheels regularly.

Equipment

When you have downtime and aren't running loads, check, repair, and clean your equipment.

Keep an inventory of all your equipment and when you purchased it. This will help you know how old it is, if something is missing, stolen, and whether you have a need for additional equipment.

You might even want to create a "wish list" of equipment that isn't necessarily vital to your day-to-day operations, but once you have funds freed up or find an incredible deal on the piece, you can add it to your inventory.

The Basics

In this chapter, you got a lot of information and it could have been a bit overwhelming. Take a breath. It sounds like a lot of time, money, and outlaw but it'll come together.

The basics that you need (other than your business documentation and licensing, but we're getting to that) are your truck, trailer, some straps, and ropes and you are on your way.

Are you enjoying this book so far? If so, please consider leaving a review. Even just a few words would help others decide if the book is right for them!

Chapter 3 - Insurance and Other Things You Need To Know to Get Started

As a hotshot operator, you will not have the same regulations as a Class 8 driver, but you will have some of the same things that you have to accomplish.

License

Generally, you are required to have a commercial driver's license (CDL) if you have any of the following qualifications:

- If you are pulling loads over 26,001 pounds
- You transport toxic or hazardous material
- The combined weight rating of your trailer and truck are over 26,001 pounds

Check with your individual state's requirements.

Depending on your individual situation, you may be required to drive with a CDL learner's permit for a time before taking the test. They may also require a log and evidence of practice hours behind the wheel.

In order to qualify, you must be at least 21 years old and have no disqualifying criminal records. Individual states may have further requirements, so check with your state's DMV.

You will be required to take your state's version of a skill test with a licensed examiner. You will need to show proficiency in a number of situations and use the vehicle you will be driving for work. You may be required to demonstrate braking technique, driving, and manual transmission operation if necessary.

Due to new federal restrictions, states are no longer allowed to issue temporary commercial driver's licenses. Once you pass, you will be required to wait for your license before you can legally drive commercially.

While you may find that your state does not require you to obtain a commercial driver's license, other states that you travel to may have different laws. So, if you are going to be traveling over state lines in the future, it will probably be worth it to get that CDL to make sure you are always on the right side of the law.

DOT and Motor Carrier Numbers

If you are transporting cargo, you are required to have the Department of Transportation and Motor Carrier Authority numbers.

The DOT number is used to follow your company's safety record and make sure that you have fulfilled all safety requirements and regulations. Your DOT number will be used to identify you on reports, safety inspections, crash investigations, and reviews.

The motor carrier number is used to identify the type of trucking business you operate and what types of goods and freight you are allowed to haul.

In order to secure these numbers, you will need to fill out the Motor Carrier Identification Report (MCS-150) and a Safety Certification Application.

Visit the Federal Motor Carrier Safety Administration website for application information.

Unified Carrier Registration

If you transport over state or international borders, you will be required to register for the Unified Carrier Registration (UCR) and pay an annual fee. The fee is based on the size of your trucking fleet, so as a hotshotter, it will be on the low end.

The program was partially created to make sure that trucks have active insurance in every state that they travel in. Registration occurs using your DOT and MC numbers. For more information, contact the Department of Transportation in your state.

International Registration Plan Tag (IRP)

This is a special plate that allows you to operate in all states and most Canadian provinces. You need to pay a fee.

DOT Physical and Drug Test

If the weight of your combined vehicles is over 10,001 pounds, you will be required to get a DOT physical and carry your medical certificate while operating your truck.

There are several restrictions that will keep you from passing:

- If you have diabetes and are required to take injectable insulin.
- You have less than 20/40 vision but do not have glasses or contacts to correct it.
- You fail the DOT drug test

You will be asked about your health history including any strokes, heart attacks, hearing loss, kidney disease, or psychiatric disorders. Once you pass, your certificate will be valid for two years.
You will also be required to take a DOT urine drug test. That tests for marijuana, cocaine, amphetamines, opioids, and

PCP. You can also be required to take a drug test after an accident or returning to work after an extended absence. But those are usually employer-based decisions.

Insurance

The FMCSA requires you carry at least $750,000 in primary liability insurance. This is going to cost you anywhere between $6,000 and $12,000 a year for a single truck and trailer. The actual cost will be based on your state, driving history, type of truck, deductible, and other factors.

You may be required to submit to the insurance company a drug and alcohol test based upon your state laws and policy. You will also be required to file information on service hours, certifications, and other qualifications.

You will also need to carry cargo insurance. The legal minimum is $5,000 but your clients are most likely going to feel safer with a higher amount. You will probably want to invest in $100,000 of cargo coverage. Some specific loads may require you to get additional insurance.

If you have multiple loads at the same time, you may be required to have separate policies to cover each piece of freight. Contact your insurance carrier for more information.

You may want to consider different quotes for different loads. For example, if you normally only carry loads valued at under $10,000, then you can stay at that level. If you have an opportunity to haul something with a much higher value, then you can temporarily upgrade your insurance for that load and reestablish your original setting after it's safely delivered.

You are going to also want to get physical damage coverage (collision and comprehensive) for your truck and trailer so if something happens, you can get them fixed and back on the road as soon as possible.

Background Check

Under certain circumstances including cross state lines and transporting certain materials, you may need a federal background check. It might be a good idea to have one on file, just in case.

Contact the Transportation Security Administration to schedule an appointment.

Training & Certification

Depending on the laws of your individual state, you may be required to complete training certification classes in order to take the CDL test. Contact your local DMV for more information.

There is numerous truck driving schools that offer training classes for hotshot trucks. Depending on your level of experience, taking one of these courses to learn the basics or as a refresher course might be a good idea. It's never too late to stop learning.

Also, check with your insurance company about a safe driver and trained driver discounts. Spending a few hundred dollars on a safety course could save you much more than that over time on your insurance rates.

Running a Business

One of the best options for you as you create the business side of your hotshot company is setting up a limited liability company or LLC. Opening an LLC provides you with a number of advantages and safety nets as a business owner.

It protects you from any personal liability and creates a limited liability through the business. You will also be issued a Federal Employer Identification Number which is like a social security number for your business. You will need this for opening bank accounts or any transactions with your state government.

You are not required to file a corporate tax return; however, you will be required to file with your state. Creating an LLC also gives you financial options such as a business including lines of credit, loans, and business rate credit cards. These are based upon your Federal EIN and the credit you are building through your company.

Laws and fees vary by state and you aren't even required to open the LLC in the state you reside or operate in. However, you are required to have a registered agent in that state.

You can open an LLC on your own by filing paperwork with your state, but it is highly advised that you bring in either an attorney or a registration company to handle the paperwork. A lawyer will cost more than a registration company, so the final decision is up to you. However, after you create your LLC, you will have to follow through with your state government as to any further fees or documents that require filing.

Often, companies will create their LLC in a state that has lower taxes or fees, but you must have a physical address and a person who works with you in that state. Many LLC registration companies can provide the registered agent and some will include it in the cost of filing for the first year.

Do I Need a Post Office Box?

This is a bit of a tricky one due to modern advances in technology.

There was a time when you would get a post office box for your business and all mail would be sent there. However, in the 21st century, in a response to money laundering, terrorism, and other illegal activities, laws began to change and not allow P.O. boxes as an address for filings or bank accounts.

Soon, thereafter, mailbox stores began to offer "non p.o. box" addresses or addresses with an actual street number. So, you could still get a mailbox, but your address would be accepted by banks and government offices.

However, with the expansion of data software and address databases, banks soon started searching addresses and can tell if an address is actually a mailbox center and will reject the address. Many credit card companies will also not allow you to use a mailbox for your address and put it through the same process.

You can use your home address on your filings and your business bank account. If you decide to get a mail or P.O. Box, you can use it for other information and mailings, but all in all, it's really going to be money you don't need to spend.

Do I Need A Home Office?

Short answer, yes. Long answer, what do you mean by the office?

When you are not on the road, you are going to need an area to do paperwork, fill out forms, even just have phone meetings. How big of an area you need is up to you. If you just want to use your kitchen table, that can work, but you'll find that you can outgrow it quite quickly. You may have an extra room in your home or even just a corner desk, but that's your office. If you decide to operate as an individual, you may be able to deduct your home office on your taxes.

Or you may need to actually rent a space. You would probably have a few drivers under you by this point as well as an operations manager of some type. Beyond that, your home office will probably suffice for a time to come.

Another question is about hiring a type of operations manager. Often, spousal teams will operate the business together with one doing runs and the other back at base answering calls, paying bills, and taking care of other office work.

You may decide to hire someone to serve in this capacity and be your operations manager (or a title of your choosing).

Make sure that they are someone you can trust and have interviewed and checked into references.

Banking

If you decide to create an LLC (which I strongly advise) and you receive your paperwork and EIN number, you can open a checking account at the bank of your choice. You'll need to bring in all documentation from your filing in order to do so.

Your regular bank might be right for you as a natural extension of your personal account. However, you may want to shop around to make sure that you use a bank that can handle your business needs. Schedule an appointment with one of their business customer service reps and discuss what they have to offer.

Try to find an account with online services as well as one that doesn't charge a service fee if you keep a minimum balance. Also, make sure they are an easily accessible bank because especially in the first few months of operation, you will be dealing with them a lot.

Business License

According to your local laws, you may need a business license since you are operating under their auspices. Consult your local city hall or government offices about any requirements.

Budgeting

You are going to need to budget for your hotshotting business. However, just starting out is going to be difficult because mostly everything is going to be theoretical. After a few years, you will have a much better idea of how much the actual cost of things will be but the first year will be difficult. Don't create any cash issues if items start to become higher than you expected. This is where your contingency funds come in. A suggestion of ten to fifteen percent is standard, but you may find yourself pushing through that.

Fixed Costs vs. Variable Costs

As an owner-operator, you are going to face two types of costs. The first type is fixed costs. These are the costs that are not going to change and are usually due on the same time on a monthly or annual basis.

These can include:

Truck and Trailer Payments

If you have payments on a truck, then it's easy to know what your monthly requirements will be and budget accordingly. However, depending on your operational setup, your pay has payments on trailers as well. Always be aware of when payments are due and how long is left in your payment plan. If you have an older truck and you are spending a lot of money on repairs, it might be time to consider something newer. If you are spending more on keeping your old rig on the road than a monthly payment would cost, it's probably time to go truck shopping. Do some research into the payments and figure out what is right for you.

Insurance Premiums

You will know your annual, bi-annual, quarterly, or monthly payment schedule for your insurance premiums. If possible, try to negotiate a better rate for your insurance by paying it off in full annually or every six months. Always be looking for cheaper coverage at the end of your term.

You can also lower your rates by:

- Raising your deductible if you are able to handle the amount.
- Make sure the policy is right for you and doesn't have extras you don't need.

- Ask about discounts for truckers, safe driving, AAA, etc.
- If you don't leave your state or only operate within a certain distance of your home base, ask about the radius of operation discounts.

Medical Premiums

You need to have health insurance. So, factor this into your budget. You may be able to find less expensive policies through your business.

Annual Licenses and Registrations

Every state has vehicle inspections, registrations, and testing as well as your driver's license or any renewal fees.

Depending on local laws, you may need business licenses or certifications. Make sure you keep up on all of your expiration dates. Contact your local government offices for requirements.

Memberships and Affiliations

There may be certain associations and guilds that will be helpful. Roadside assistance programs, civic groups, chambers of commerce, and such will all have dues. Some of them may have lifetime membership rates that will save you money.

Load Boards

Later, we'll talk more about online load boards and apps. These are vital to your work and many of them charge a monthly or annual fee. So, make sure you calculate this into your budget.

Office Space and Supplies

Do you have an office? Don't forget the costs of operating there when you aren't on the road. Calculate utilities, rent, office supplies, and other costs. Also, be aware of any local business license requirements.

If it is your home office, make sure you keep track of the same information to deduct on your personal taxes. Also, be aware of any local regulations regarding operations of the business in a residence. This can also include the storage of your rig at your home.

Variable Costs

These are the things you need to budget for, but can easily change based upon the number of miles you drive as well as due to circumstances beyond your control.

These can include:

Truck and Trailer Maintenance

Your truck is going to need maintenance inside and out. So, you'll need to budget for regular service visits and repairs. Don't forget tires! It's often left off the list. Keeping on top of tire maintenance and replacing them regularly can lead to savings not only in truck repairs but also help save you from downtime and lost income.

And don't forget the cost of washing and cleaning supplies if you're going to keep your truck spotless.

Fuel

This is the one that can hurt the most. In the current market, fuel prices can also spike very quickly as well as have wide cost variations from state to state.

Look for any way you can to save on fuel costs. Bonus programs, reward cards, and mobile apps will help.

Lodging

Some of your runs will require you to stay in a motel or hotel. You may not be able to calculate how often this happens, but you'll need to make a budget allowance for it.

On the road, look into travel and lodging apps to get the best rates and to help you stay within your budget. Some apps offer rewards programs leading to free hotel nights. Make sure you also take advantage of any loyalty programs for hotel or motel chains.

Food on the Road

Eating on the road adds up quick. Be realistic about how much food can cost, and remember, often prices on the highway are higher. Also, take into account water, coffee, and snack allowances to keep in the cab while you are on the road.

Make sure you save all those receipts for any qualifying tax deductions.

Professional Services

You may be the boss, but you are probably going to need some help. You may need to hire a bookkeeper or accountant who does charge fees. But in the end, you will end up saving money and avoid some major headaches. Also, budget for tax preparation services. You may have other office workers, janitorial staff, or truck maintenance employees you need to add to your payroll budget.

Allow for any sort of skills or training courses that you take. These types of safety courses may give you discounts on insurance policies or certification processes. Contact your insurance provider for more information.

Software

Even with someone doing your books, you may still need software for your operation.

If you are using software, it is highly advised that you budget for licenses and subscriptions versus downloading pirated versions. As a small business owner, it just isn't worth the risk of fines or computer viruses.

Communications

You'll need to keep in touch on the road so you'll have a phone/data bill. Roaming plans can vary by state and country depending on the carrier. Always make sure to look for the plan that's right based on your travel. Compare the shops to find the plan that's right for you and your operation.

There are some great smartphone apps out there to help you with navigation, scheduling, invoicing, and other trucking needs. Many of them are free, but often, the pro versions are worth the fee; however, they can add up.

Parking and Tolls

Not only might you have costs for parking while at your home base, but you might also require parking while on the road.

Depending on where you drive in the country, tolls might be something you need to include in your budget. Look into EZ passes and other programs for potential discounts.

Taxes

Depending on how you are set up as a business, you can have a number of different taxes from personal taxes to LLCs to corporations to local business taxes.

Use a professional tax preparer to make sure that you get every possible deduction and your returns are put together properly.

Your Payroll

Don't forget that you need to get paid. Include your own salary in your budget. If you hire other drivers or staff, you will, of course, need to pay them. You may need to look into a payroll service to handle processing checks and taking care of payroll taxes.

You may also face other expenses

Business Development

Growing your business is important for an operation of any size, even yours. So depending on how you need to market your services, factor in some money for websites, advertisements, and promotions. Online directories may charge fees for listings as well.

These services can run from $100 for a simple website to thousands of dollars based upon your operation's professional needs. You can also hire someone to run your social media or prepare billboards, commercials, or online ads.

Specialty E

If you drive a refrigerated truck or have other specialty deliveries, don't forget to take this into account. Also, consider the cost of maintaining and replacing straps, winches, and other gear for flatbed trailers.

A Contingency Plan

Stuff happens. Tickets, accidents, longer than expected runs, breakdowns. Cost overruns are a fact of life for small businesses. Don't budget yourself so tight you can't handle a surprise.

Cost Per Mile

Using all this information, you can estimate your cost per mile. The goal is to get that number as low as possible to maximize profitability for your operation.

Add all your cost estimates (fixed and variable costs) and divide by the number of miles you think you will cover. That'll give you your estimated cost per mile.

So, for example, if you calculated you had $100,000 in total fixed and variable annual expenses and planned on covering 75,000 miles next year:

100,000 operating expenses/75,000 miles = 1.33 cents a mile

If you want to increase profitability, you can lower your costs or raise your miles (although some costs will go up accordingly). Once you get on the road, you may find that your numbers were way off, but it gives you the ability to begin to plan. As you get to know your own operation, it will become more concrete and you are on your way to a successful operation.

Credit Cards

If you get credit cards for your business, look for ones with fuel incentives. Whether extra points, discounts, or cash back, if you stay ahead on payments, you will end up ahead since fuel is one of your major costs. Points can be used for cash back, gift cards, and ironically, more fuel.

Where Do I Open My Business?

Your first instinct is to open your business where you live. It makes sense, that's where you would want to work right?

Well, depending on your situation, you might want to consider other options.

As you start to research your business, look at load boards and see how many jobs and how many hotshotters are in your area. If it's a possibility, you might want to consider opening your business somewhere else.

For example, Texas and Georgia are two of the areas that have the largest amount of hotshot truckers. You might think this is because there's a huge demand and it would be the best place to open up shop.
However, the opposite is true. That means that the market is flooded and it's going to be difficult to get the mileage rate you want because there is so much competition they are going to be fighting for the gigs.

You might consider opening up or driving in areas that are underserved. If you are serious about growing a legitimate trucking business and eventually adding more routes or drivers, you might want to open up in another town or even another state.

Partnering

Partnering is different from hiring an employee. Partnering is bringing in another individual to assist with driving and other tasks. They take on part of the risk for a share of the profits. Depending on your arrangement, they may take on financial responsibility legally in the company or LLC. If this is the case, consult an attorney to draw up paperwork and explain how it works.

It's up to you how you would arrange partnering, but most often, it's to have two drivers in a single rig so you can drive longer hours by switching off but also have a second set of hands for loading, which can make the process much safer and easier.

Be careful before partnering with anyone. Make sure the action comes from a business mind and not a place of emotion. Often, people partner with friends or family members to help them out or they think it will be fun, not because they bring skills or experience to the table.

Also, make sure you document the partnership and be clear about responsibilities and obligations. Everyone should know how much their cut is, what goes back into the company, and how you plan on moving forward as a business.

Never just "bring someone in" without making sure that they are certified and licensed. If something happens and they aren't legal, it's your name on the fines, and the business that might be lost is yours.

Charity

Part of being a well-rounded business can be giving back to your community and others. Yes, if you give cash, you will receive tax deductions but it can be a rewarding experience and doesn't always have to be about money.

Because of the unique service that you offer with your rig, you can help out with charities that need assistance.

By giving them a few hours of your time, you can save them a great deal of badly needed funds.

Try to find an organization that means something to you so you make a connection with their cause. You will be more rewarded since you are helping something that is meaningful to you.

Charitable giving and volunteer service is also a great way to network and it is some free advertising, but the important part is helping. You have an opportunity to do some good along with your success and give back.

Chapter 4 - How to Get Freight

When you are first starting out, you are going to need to be hustling to get jobs. And when you are more experienced, you are still going to need to hustle. And did I mention that you are always going to need to be hustling to find jobs?

It's not deterrence; it's just the nature of the business. Those loads and jobs are out there, some are good and some are bad, but you need to go find them. Work isn't going to come knocking on your door.

How much per mile?

In the last chapter, we discussed how you can figure out your cost per mile. While many hotshot truckers say their costs are around 80 to 85 cents per mile (compared with a Class 8 which can be 1.25 to 1.50 or more). You will need to figure out your own budget in order to discover what your cost is per mile.

When you bid for loads, you are going to need to offer a flat rate bid for the job or a cost per mile. Most likely, hotshotters are going to be bidding in the range of $1.00 to $1.50 per mile, but of course, this depends on the locations, type of freight, duration, time of day, distance from your home base, need for cash, and other factors.

It is vital that you understand your bottom line finances before you begin to bid on loads. You don't want to bid so low that you get the job but actually lose money by taking it. This is a very easy way to quickly destroy your business and go under.

You'll also need to take into consideration the location and weather. It may only be a few miles, but if it's over gravel or unpaved roads or into the wilderness, you aren't going to be able to turnaround as quick for the next load, or worse, you may get lost or held up by terrain and the rest of your hotshotting day is gone.

The same goes with the weather. In bad weather, it may take you longer to deliver freight due to the elements or traffic being backed up. If a load doesn't offer enough incentive and you are on the fence about whether you are going to make money, make sure you give the gig a lot of thought before signing up.

However, you will need to decide, sometimes, if getting some money is better than none. You may have a day when the only gig you can get doesn't quite cover the mileage, but you need to bring in something. You may decide that cash in hand is better than nothing. It's the problem with being the boss…you have to make the decision.

The Hotshot Load Boards

One of the best ways to get freight and keep yourself on the road to making money is the Hotshot boards.

There are dozens of these websites and some are definitely better and more concise than others. However, it's also a personal choice and how it relates to your company. Some boards may list jobs that are more your style and right for your rig setup, while others may list jobs that aren't right in content, weight, or distance. Others may be more regional and depend on your location.

There are different types. Some are simple listings almost like classified ads with requests, location, pay offered, and miles. Others are more automated and interactive.

Get to know all the boards and learn which ones are going to be the most successful for you. Make sure to talk to other drivers and listen and learn from their experiences with the different board services.

Some websites have grown to the point where they offer apps and haul and payment management. This adds to your ability to keep picking up loads because you can be getting ready for your next one as you are unloading your current cargo.

Every board is a bit different, but they will have various information including rates of comparable small trucking companies, messaging boards, and days-to-pay information.

Be careful when dealing with boards that you are not familiar with. You need to always keep one eye open in business dealings with people you haven't worked with before.

Free Boards vs. Paid Boards

As I mentioned earlier, you'll need to explore the load boards and figure out which one is right for you and your setup. The best place to start is the free boards as you navigate your way through the hotshot trucking world.

You'll be able to figure out how it works and build your skillset. Then look into the paid boards, many of which will allow you to try their services before joining. Fees can range from $30 to over $100 a month. They will offer different loads and services.

However, you don't need to sign up for every board out there. In fact, you might spend all your profits just trying to find more work. Investigate which boards are right for you and invest in them.

Make sure you fill out all the information in your company profile. Potential customers want to see that you are professional and your profile is where they can learn all about you. Be honest, but put your best foot forward.

Tell them about your experience, your truck(s), your location, and what type of freight you haul. Also, don't forget to mention how far you will or won't travel for loads.

Also, don't get greedy. All too often, new drivers take on multiple loads and suddenly realize they have overextended themselves. Keep a close track of the location and time of your loads.

Some of the load boards also offer the opportunity to learn about industry standards, practices, trends, and new potential clients. Many of the sites also offer messaging services so you can speak directly with potential clients to answer any questions you might have about a gig.

Some services even offer matching services that will alert you about potential jobs or interested clients.

Tips for Using Load Boards

- Don't just pay for every board at first. Use free trials and decide which boards are right for you before laying out too much capital. Those fees can add up quickly.
- Put your best foot forward when it comes to your company (and not just on the load boards). Be honest, but describe yourself in a positive manner. Consider a professionally-designed logo. The more information a potential client has about you, the more likely they will hire you.
- Don't stray from your minimum. Always be aware of how much you could gain or lose from a load.
- Be patient. Don't rush a transaction and also don't jump on a load that looks problematic or low paying from a place of fear or anxiety.
- Many of the sites have alerts and notifications for loads that match your criteria. Use them!
- Be concerned about your reputation. Every load, big or small, is a representation of your work ethic. Treat every piece of freight as important.
- Don't overbook your freight. Make sure you have enough time and energy to give each load the attention it deserves. The last thing you want is an unhappy customer because you are behind schedule.
- Be ready to negotiate in both directions. Not only will you need to drop your price sometimes, but you should also be ready to negotiate a higher rate if the market or the item supports more pay.
- Some load boards will have tools that will allow you to chart the availability of trucks and loads, so you can track supply and demand and set your rates accordingly.

Contracts

While using the load boards and working on a load by load basis is one way to hotshot, it's going to be a difficult way to sustain your business. You should be looking for opportunities to get regular customers and contracts. It doesn't mean you are giving up your freedom, but knowing you have a few guaranteed deliveries a week sure helps support your bottom line.

You may be able to secure a regular delivery with a company you work with frequently or pick up parts of a regular delivery route. It's up to you to find the opportunities though.

Always read contracts carefully and ask any questions you may have. Make sure that the contract doesn't put any stipulations on you as a business owner such as non-complete clauses, fees, fines, or anything else that you are not happy with. It's fine to ask for an addition to a contract.

Deadheading

Deadheading is when you drive to or from one of your destinations with an empty trailer. Any time you are driving somewhere without a load, they're deadhead miles. And deadhead miles are losing you money.

This is why you are constantly working the boards for new opportunities. Always look for that return load. If it doesn't go all the way back to home base or your next pickup, it's worth it. Even if it's out of the way but you still end up closer to home, it's a win.

There are times when it may pay to wait for a bit after dropping off a load to see if you can find freight for your return trip. However, don't spend your whole day waiting. You may miss other loads closer to home base that you could have taken or you may wait too long and find your short trip home is suddenly much longer because you are now caught in rush-hour traffic.

There are other concerns besides just the financial one. Empty trailers can be difficult to control at times, such as during heavy weather. It can bounce around violently, potentially causing damage to the trailer and the truck.

Also, for any DOT logs, you are still technically "on duty," so you need to log the trip and that you are empty.

Minimum Load Rate

We all have that friend who goes to Vegas, promises that he has a limit and blows through all the money, and then he spends a little more. And a little more. And a little more.

Be careful that does not become the story of your minimum load rate.

As you are bidding on your loads or making deals, you need to calculate what your minimum load rate will be. Earlier, we discussed how to calculate your per mile cost. Use this information to calculate the lowest amount that you can take per mile. Many hotshotters set theirs between 1.25 and 1.50 a mile, but every situation is different.

Think of it like this—take your cost per mile; let's say it's a dollar, for easy math. You have a potential load that will pay you $500 to drive 100 miles. That means the trip is going to cost you $100 so you will make $400.

However, take your deadhead cost into consideration. It still costs fuel, wear and tear on your truck, and time to return without another load, and you can't guarantee you'll always have one. If you have multiple options, always take potential deadhead returns into consideration. One job may seem to pay more but when you factor in other costs, you may find it's actually a potential loser compared to a shorter run. In our example above, the true cost is actually $200 because your costs still come in around a dollar a mile on the way back. That's why it's so important to not deadhead and find more loads.

So, remember that Vegas friend of yours? This is where we revisit his approach to limits. Some load board apps and websites will have a running online "auction" where you can lower your bids. Or you may feel like you are losing a person-to-person negotiation and feel you should drop your price. You can drop it but realize you are losing money. If getting some is better than nothing, that's understandable. But make sure that's true. Make sure you are constantly doing the math with an understanding of how much you have to make or lose on any load.

Freight Factoring

Often, you may wait 30-60 days to receive the payment for your load. It might be due to the load board you use or because you have invoiced the customer, and legally, they have time to pay the invoice.

In order to get cash into your account quicker, some drivers will use freight factoring. This is where the owner uses a separate company to handle the invoice.

For example, if you hauled a classic car and made $5,000, you would invoice your client and send a copy to a freight factoring service. They would then advance you the amount of the invoice minus a small fee, usually between two and five percent.

While it is not the perfect solution, it can work as a great way for you to get money moving while you are still starting out.

Some freight factor companies will also help with fuel advances. However, make sure you read all of the fine print and understand exactly what you are signing, and what any fees or costs might be.

Freight Seasons

Even aside from downturns in the economy or manufacturing, trucking can be seasonal and cyclical. You need to be prepared for these leaner times and become inventive at finding jobs while keeping costs down and putting aside funds.

During the fall and winter, the amount of runs goes down. Companies tend to slow down as the holidays begin to arrive and aren't sending out as many shipments. Yes, there are special holiday shipments, but they aren't going to be as regular as freight normally is the rest of the year. Plus, obviously, weather plays a factor in it.

The heavy season for freight is generally from April to October. During those months, you have the best chance to log a lot of loads and also at higher rates. During this time, you should not only be paying your bills but putting funds away for the leaner winter months in case you can't hit your freight targets.

Advertising

While the boards are going to be one of your main ways to find freight, you don't want to discount other traditional forms of advertising.

Make sure you display your business name and contact information on your truck and trailer. Put in the time and money to do it properly. You want people who see your rig to know that you are professional and the way you display it will show them. Use a clean font with a phone number, website, and email. Make sure the information is easy to see and read. Try not to use strange emails with numbers or funny names that will be difficult for people to remember or to understand.

Online

Marketing yourself online is almost a necessity in this day and age. However, it is nowhere near as difficult or expensive as many business owners believe.

Website

The best place to begin is with a business website. Here you can give out all your business basic details about location, the distance you'll travel, information on your truck(s), and contact info. People will be able to learn more about you and your business which will help them feel more secure about letting you handle their precious cargo.

You can design your own website with various companies for only a few dollars a month using simple and clear templates. If you want something unique and different, you can hire a designer to create your site. However, realize a designer is going to run you a few thousand dollars by the time all is said and done and you might have been able to get the same result on your own for a few hundred annually.

It might be worth it to hire someone to handle your SEO (search engine optimization). What this means is that they would make sure all the seen and unseen (meta tags) text on your website is written in a way that will best be picked up by search engines and other online bots.

You also want to make sure you are listed in company directories and that you encourage clients to leave reviews.

Depending on the size of your business, you might want to consider a social media manager. They can handle everything from social media posts and keeping up with your online presence to press releases and even some customer interaction. Their services fees vary but usually they are between $300 and $1,000 a month.

Social Media

Thought by many to be the place for cat videos and silly memes, the realm of social media can be very valuable to your business.

There are different avenues for a social media presence to be built on, so don't be afraid to experiment with different ones. However for a trucking business, the following is probably your best option to focus on:

Photo-Based Sharing Platforms

For the most part, a photo-based social media platform will allow you to share photos of your truck, cargo, and travels and develop a following. By using pictures, you can engage your audience and potential clients with an inside look at what your business does.

By updating regularly and interacting with followers and commenters, you will not only be connected with potential clients but meet other hotshot truckers and learn from their experiences. While some of them may be competition, it can be friendly and you can both learn from each other.

Many small businesses have found success on social media by posting non work-related things. Positive memes, travel photos, and funny happenings caught on the road can be very effective in bringing in new followers and potential clients. Consider life on the road pictures, strange street signs, or sights. The basic rule of thumb is that if you find it interesting and cool, someone else out there will as well.

Social Media Ads

This is a tricky one. Some businesses are very reliant on ads saying they see huge spikes in customer interaction, while others have never done anything with them. It's really up to you and be sure to do your own business research.

While spending money on targeted social media ads can reach out to potential clients, it can be a waste of money for hotshotters because their clients are probably not looking on social media for immediate hire. They are going to brokers and load boards.

Brand recognition is a term you might hear thrown around as well. Some people say that it's important to get your name and brand out there so when people do need to hire someone to move their freight, they'll remember you and call you up with your next gig. The problem is, you aren't selling a soft drink that you want them to remember the next time they are thirsty, which will occur far more often then them needing a load shipped.

When someone needs your services, unless they ship on a daily basis, the odds they will remember an ad for a service they didn't need are very low. And even if they remember your ad, they may not remember your name or other information and just end up hiring the first business they come across in a directory or they'll go to a load board and you have to bid like everyone else.

So, you need to decide if it's the right decision to spend the money, and most likely, it's not.

Networking

There's often an approach in business that all others are competitors and should be treated with disdain. However, quite often, treating other businesses in the same industry with respect and befriending them can lead to your benefit.

By networking with other drivers, you not only can learn things about the business, but you make contacts. There might be times when a driver can't take a gig and he might call you to see if you can take it on. You can make contacts for jobs. Not to mention, it's just nice to socialize with people who are in the same business and know the things you are going through.

It doesn't just have to be in person, either. Using social media to connect with other drivers and business owners is an easy way to network.

Business Cards and Other Print Support

There was a time when the only thing a trucker had to advertise was the yellow pages, the phone number on the side of his truck, and word of mouth. Now, that has changed, but there is still a place for some old forms of advertising including the good old-fashioned business card.

With the proliferation of print shops and online services, getting business cards has become an incredibly simple and inexpensive thing to do. Make sure you order business cards and keep a generous amount in your truck and on yourself.

When you order them, make sure it has your entire basic information—company name, your name, phone number, and email. Don't put your home address on the card, even if that is your place of business.

Make sure the card looks clean and professional. It's okay to use a cool picture of a truck and trailer or other design but don't clog it up with images, logos, or cartoony clip art. Stay professional and informative.

It's also more affordable than ever to have professional looking postcards and flyers printed up. You may decide to do a targeted mailing of postcards or it's just as great to have them left at high traffic locations. Doing a mass mailing to every house or business in town is probably not a great idea, and honestly, a waste of time and money. The vast majority of the people you reach are not going to need your services and the card will just end up going into the trash. But if you research your targets, you'll be spending your money in a much wiser fashion. You can also purchase mailing lists from businesses in your area or of a certain type so you can manage your mailing campaign.

You might decide to leave some at an exotic car show for people who might need your services. Or possibly, at a rodeo if you work with horses. By just having them with you, you'll find opportunities to leave them in places that will help create business leads. Make sure the postcards are clean looking with your contact information easily readable.

Flyers can be helpful as well but always ask before posting or leaving at a business or establishment.

Email Campaign

Some small business owners will create an email campaign to advertise their services and get their name out to the community. This can work really well or it can quickly backfire and cause major headaches for you and your business.

If you send out too many emails, your server or ISP may actually throttle your account due to the data being sent out.

The gatekeeping software will assume you are spamming and shut you down. Or your ISP may receive a complaint that you are spamming from one of your addresses. Even if you don't consider what you are doing to be spamming, a couple of complaints and your ISP will shut you down.

Often, business owners will turn to mailing list services. However, they will only send emails out to people who you know or who opt-in for the mailings. You will be banned from the services if you try to work around this.
Now, this can be a great service once you have clients. Ask them to join your mailing list and keep up with your business. If you do this, make sure the information you send out is important and relevant. Use stories from your runs, photographs, facts, and discounts. However, don't inundate them with emails. Once or twice a month is fine, but don't send your list an email every day.

If you do decide to do your own email campaign from your own computer, do it carefully and with forethought. Make sure your email is clean, concise, and informative. Don't make it sound or look like a form email, or their email system will spam it before it even gets in front of your potential client. Don't use large attachments.

If someone responds to you to take them off your list, do it. You don't want word getting around that your business is a spammer.

Only send out emails in bursts. Don't send them out hundreds at a time or this will clog your ISP and you may get banned or frozen. Also, don't send it out to a big list of "undisclosed" people using BCC. This will trigger spam controls with your intended recipient and it will get trashed.

Getting Paid

On the load boards, a broker or the client will pay you. Other times, you may need to make arrangements through other services.

On the load boards, there will be information on how long it will take you to get paid. Remember, some gigs may take 30 to 60 days before you see any money while others might pay immediately. If you can't wait for payment, you might want to consider the freight factoring we discussed.

If you are doing a load that you negotiated through another source or personally, then you will need to get paid in cash, check, or credit card. You also have to invoice them and wait for a check or other payment.

Consider getting a credit card reader for payment. You can use services that turn your smartphone into a credit card reader and you're all set for a small fee. Always be wary of taking checks from individuals and even some companies. Call the bank to verify the account before accepting.

Look for the Niches

You will make the most money if you are open to the most types of loads. However, you might be able to find a niche where you can develop clients and even cater to specific needs;

- Medical Hotshot- delivering equipment and parts for hospitals, clinics, and laboratories. Depending on what you haul, you may need to modify your trailer, but if you are able to lock in a client and numerous loads over time, it might be worth the investment.
- Agriculture- An industry that always needs new parts, replacements, equipment, and large tools and machines, this is a niche that can provide steady work.

- Perishable - Food, produce, and other items that need to get to their destination as fast as possible. Again, you may need to make modifications, but if it is because of a long-term contract, it's worth it.
- Specialty car - This industry is one where you are transporting people's lifelong dreams, so it will require a bit of a velvet glove touch. You need to make sure you can transport their vehicles in a manner that they will be pristine when delivered.
- Equestrian - It could be someone else's trailer or you might decide to invest in your own, but if you live in horse country, you could easily create niche transporting ponies. Often, the rodeo circuit in a region can be seasonal, so you might even consider renting a horse trailer for a limited amount of time and pick up jobs.
- Film production - The film industry has gone nationwide and often has last-minute emergency equipment that needs to be transported to set. Make contacts with your local film commission.

Also, don't be afraid to think out of the box. As you get to know the industry, you may see an area that needs service that isn't being provided. It might be something you know little about or it might come to your sight because it's something you already have an interest in. Always be watching and asking questions and never initially shut yourself off to opportunity. However, learn how to quickly decide if a type of contract is right for you and the client. This will save everyone headaches down the road.

You may also want to look into destinations. There might be underserved locations or destinations that are overwhelmed with need.

For example, Las Vegas has a lot of conventions that feature cars, large displays, and other big items. If you are in a position to move things to a convention center like that, then you should look into how to harness those jobs.

We've all heard the stories of the boomtowns in the Dakotas and the trucking industry on the ice roads in Alaska. If you do some research, you'll find situations where you can go to work for a limited amount of time and make a large amount of money with your truck. It's, in a way, a replay of the original hotshotters back in Texas.

Niches aren't always going to be obvious, and you may need to put several together. If you find several clients that you know have a certain number of deliveries a month and you can make arrangements to be their carrier, then you have locked in a percentage of your needed runs to hit your numbers. Then, it becomes less stressful to get the remainder you need to enter into profitability.

Signing With a Trucking Company

You may find that it isn't the right time to go out on your own with your company. In fact, you may find that you need a bit of support while you learn the ropes and bring in revenue. You have your truck and trailer, but you aren't ready to start your own business.

At this time, it might be the right choice to sign with a trucking company. This will help on several levels including the bringing in of customers. You won't have to worry about finding your next gig as you learn the ropes.

Companies will have certain requirements that can range from physicals and drug tests as well as any rules specific to their company. However, you will be able to learn more about the workings of the industry without worrying about revenue.

Some companies will provide a truck for you while others only work with drivers who have their own. Realize that if they provide the vehicle, most likely, they will take a larger percentage of the freight fees.

Logbooks

By federal law, every driver operating a commercial motor vehicle must have a logbook where they track their status and miles or have an electronic device that does this. It must include:

- Date
- Daily miles
- Vehicle number
- Carrier name
- Driver's signature
- Shipping information

You will receive further information with your DOT number application.

Appearance

We've touched on this a bit, but it's important, so let's discuss appearance a bit further.

You started your trucking company for many reasons and one of them might have been freedom. No longer did you want to have someone telling you what to wear, how to conduct business, where to be, and how to act. You wanted to be the master of your domain and do things your way.

However, as a business owner, you are quickly going to find out that all of that is about appearance and it is a vital part of your business.
There are drivers who don't care and whose truck looks like it was hauled out of a junkyard, who dress sloppily, and

address their clients like they just got off the ship during fleet week. They can be salty, smelly, and in fact, a bit rude. But they will work. They still get the job done and are making a living.

However, the chance to grow their business is escaping them because part of business growth is understanding your strengths and weaknesses and using that information to make your company bigger, stronger, and more effective. And this includes your appearance.

You don't have to wear a uniform or some other outlandish outfit, but it's important to be clean and presentable. Your client will be more relaxed about trusting you with their precious cargo and that you are going to treat it in a professional manner.

When you speak to clients (and potential clients), be pleasant, don't swear, and answer their questions truthfully and succinctly. Part of your job is to make them feel comfortable when they interact with you.

The same rules go for your truck. If your truck looks misused, clients are going to be concerned that you will treat their freight with the same attitude. Again, you may not lose the gig, but do you think that the client is going to sing your praises on review sites or to their friends or family?

Keep your truck clean and in good repair. If you have any major dents or bodywork, try to get it fixed as quickly as possible. Keep your cab clean because you never know when a client might peek inside or you might need to give someone a ride.

Make sure any signage on the truck or trailer is neat, clean, and up to date. If you have peeling letters or paint, fix it immediately. Remember that you only get one chance at a first impression, so doing a little upkeep goes a long way.

Chapter 5 - What Is Life Like On the Road

The open road.

It's actually one of the parts of the trucker's job that appeals most to drivers; the lure of the open highway, with nobody looking over your shoulder, just the hum of the engine, and the horizon.

However, just because someone is away from home, it doesn't mean that there aren't things you can do to make life on the road healthier and a bit easier.

Exercise and healthy eating are incredibly important, especially for truck drivers. The amount of time spent sitting and the prevalence of an unhealthy eating and drinking lifestyle lead to a spike in heart disease and diabetes in drivers.

Truck drivers have also been shown to have higher incidents of skin cancer from the sunlight flooding into the cab for hours. Make sure you cover your arms and use sunscreen on your face and exposed skin.

What to Bring

The equipment is packed, the trailer is on, and you're ready to go... but what are the gears for you?

It depends on if you are out for the day or going to be gone for longer, but these are items you might want to consider packing for your self.

- Extra clothes and clothes to layer for warmth
- Change of clothes for when you aren't working

- Extra sunglasses
- Overnight/grooming kit (toothbrush, paste, prescriptions, razors, etc.)
- Cell phone charger
- Paperwork folder or file for load documents, receipts, and documents.
- Work gloves
- Water
- Snacks

Lodging

If you end up doing some overnights or long hauls, you are going to need to locate a motel or hotel for the night. Unlike a Class 8 rig operator, you won't have the option of sleeping in your truck.

Try to plan out your stays instead of playing it by ear on the road. If you plan your stops in advance, you can shop for the lowest rate, and thereby, save on your bottom line. And as the business owner, you know how important that is.

Also, by planning ahead, you can keep to a tighter schedule and make sure you get enough rest and food. All too often, drivers try to push themselves until they reach complete exhaustion. This can not only lead to accidents and injuries but is illegal in many states where they have laws about the number of hours you can drive on the road. Even though you may not be operating under a commercial license, drowsy driving is still illegal in most states.

Use popular hotel apps and websites to locate the best deal. Some apps offer bonus points or free night stays based upon your number of stays. Sign up for various hotel apps and compare shops.

You can also try to look for campgrounds and hostels.

Also, look into guest reward cards for the various hotel and motel chains. You may get more perks versus one you found on an app or vice versa. By spending ten minutes comparing lodgings before booking a room, you can save yourself (and your business) a nice amount of money.

And always look for that free continental breakfast!

Sleep

Getting enough sleep is important whether you are doing it at night or during the day after a night haul. But you need to get at least 7-8 hours of sleep every "night."

Lack of sleep has long-term effects that lead to diabetes, obesity, heart disease as well as your level of general comprehension and concentration. It can slow down your reaction time, which is not a good thing when you're hauling tens of thousands of pounds.

Exercise

Exercise is important for a number of reasons.

First of all, the rigors of long hours of driving can lead to injuries and muscle deterioration. As a driver, you are also at risk of back injuries. It's important to exercise and keep yourself in good shape.

Many hotels have fitness facilities that are offered as part of your stay. As you book your stays, look to see what they have to offer. If they don't have one, ask at the front desk if they have an arrangement with a nearby gym for guests.
Most gyms will offer a daily rate for a few dollars. Or if you find yourself in town for a few days, consider a weekly pass.

Another option is the national gym chains. Look into a membership with a gym that has locations in other areas that you do hotshot deliveries in. For a few extra dollars a month, you can get a membership that allows you to use multiple locations. Some gyms are open 24 hours and most have shower and locker-room facilities which can also come in handy after a long day behind the wheel.

But just because you can't find a gym, that doesn't mean it's the end of the world. Get out of your truck and stretch. Try some basic exercises to work out the kinks in your body and muscles. If nothing else, it's great to get out and clear your head from behind the wheel.

There are also small road exercise kits that include bands, weights, and other exercise equipment that you can use in the hotel room. Exercise bands are especially great because they're easy to pack and travel with and they give you access to a wide variety of exercises. And at the end of the day, you still can do bodyweight exercises such as push-ups, squats, lunges, and jumping jacks if you don't have access to any equipment.

If you are serious about losing weight, consider keeping a food diary or log. Keep track of everything you eat, when you ate, and how much you ate. Also, keep track of the calories and nutrition facts. You may have heard people refer to "tracking their macros." That's all it is, just writing down how many grams of protein, carbohydrates, sugars, and fats you are taking in.

By tracking them, you'll learn your habits and be able to figure out how to stay under your daily recommended numbers and begin to shed the pounds.

Some truckers even bring bikes or scooters with them. While your space is limited, sometimes, you might have time to get yourself moving for a quick ride while your freight is being prepared or while you wait for your next load. That type of transportation can even come in handy and save you money.

If your truck is parked in a safe zone and you want to go eat or run errands, take the scooter or bike and save on gas and the chore of parking.

Food

When it comes to food, there are multiple issues that affect your performance on the road and your life in general.

To begin, consider skipping fast food unless it's your only option. While you will be expending calories loading and unloading your trailer and freight, many hours will be spent sedentary behind the wheel. You still need to worry about what you are eating.

Try to find healthier options while stopping to eat. Avoid processed, fried foods when you can. Do your best to supplement your diet with green vegetables, fruits, and lean meat.

However, there will be times when your only options are the usual fast food restaurants at the end of a freeway off-ramp. What do you do?

Look for options. Most fast food restaurants have begun to offer healthier options such as non-fried foods and salads.

Also, look for truck stops, family restaurants, or just healthier establishments in general. Inquire about how the food is cooked and what they used to make it. Don't feel out of place. You are putting it into your body, you have every right to know what it is and how it was prepared.

Yet, there will be times when you don't need to stop but you do need something to keep you going. So, bring healthy easily consumable snacks to keep in your cab.

Consider a cooler to keep in the cab with you. There are several compact ones on the market that have an electronic plug you can attach into your cigarette lighter or auxiliary power to keep your snacks nice and cool.

- Water- Always bring plenty of water. It's a great and healthy way to quench your thirst, not to mention, you'll be thankful if you have a breakdown, especially in the desert.
- Protein and energy bars- There are many tasty brands on the market. It's important to keep your energy levels up while driving.
- Vegetables and fruit- If you are going on a short run of a day or two, consider bringing a selection of sliced-up vegetables for easy eating. Carrots, celery, radishes, berries, and melons are all great options.
- Hard-boiled eggs- A perfect snack that will keep in your cooler for several days. However, you will probably want to peel them in advance.
- Jerky- The classic truckers' treat. However, be aware of high sodium levels, especially if you have any outstanding heart or blood pressure issues.
- Protein drinks- Protein drinks are an easy way to get your nutrients on the road. You can purchase them in pre-made cans and bottles or get a bag or your own powder and make them yourself with a shaker cup and cold water.

Things to avoid

Overly sugary food- Not only is it going to affect your waistline, eating too much sugar, especially when you aren't actively moving or exercising can cause blood sugar issues to rise and, in the short term, lead to fatigue, lack of concentration, moodiness, irritability, and a general loss of quality of work. In the long run, too much sugar and processed food can lead to diabetes and other health issues.

Power and energy drinks– Often, these drinks are used as a sort of nutrition supplement, which is not their intended use. If you look at the cans, most will say limit to a certain number per day, but all too often, drinkers will down many times that number in a day.

Energy drinks can lead to insomnia, heart palpitations, and stomach and digestive issues. Studies have also shown that people who already have health issues are at an incredibly elevated risk of further issues, especially related to heart and blood pressure.

Low blood sugar and concentration issues can be a major problem on long haul drives. Consider setting an alarm on your watch or phone for every couple of hours to make sure you eat something. It's difficult, sometimes, we get in that mindset of moving steadily forward and just forget to eat. This is one way to help with that.

Entertainment

Entertainment for drivers has changed monumentally over just the last few decades. Gone are the realm of CB radio, eight tracks, and static AM radio. Now, drivers have a near endless supply of options to keep them company in the cab as they make their way down the highway.

Music

There are numerous options including satellite radio and streaming services in addition to your own digital collection. You always have good old-fashioned terrestrial radio with music, news, and talk radio.

If you are a fan of radio and have traveled through the sparser areas of the country, you know how the stations tend to fade out and leave you with limited options so be ready to turn over to your music collection. There are now areas that have set up repeaters with popular stations that broadcast in such areas as the highway systems in Nevada and Eastern California.

If you are ever on a cross-country haul, try listening to the news on the hour as you make your way down the highway. Usually, there is at least one major story playing out on the radio. You'll start to make connections with it when certain parts of the story happen with locations along your route. It's also interesting to hear different takes on news stories from different regions.

While you definitely don't want to wear them while driving, consider getting a pair of heavy-duty sound canceling headphones. For those times when you just need to relax, they'll come in very handy, plus you can use them while watching digital video media.

AudioBooks

No longer do you need a set of a dozen cassette tapes to listen to an audiobook, you can now download or stream them from various sites.

You can download fiction and non-fiction books on endless subjects. You can even binge-listen the entire collection of an author. There are also streaming sites that offer audiobooks that you can listen to.

There are also dramatic tellings of stories that you can listen to, a staple for cross-country truckers. Usually ranging from six to 10 hours, these productions feature full-cast productions with sound effects and music. Much closer to a movie than a book, they are available online and are found in truck stops across the country on CD. They offer action, westerns, dramas, and books based on well-known comics. All can be streamed through an app, downloaded as files, or purchased as CDs.

Podcasts

Podcasts are a great way to pass the time on the road. There are endless topics from news and current events to comedy and drama, sports, investigative journalism, and education. They can be downloaded through the service of your choice.

Streaming Video

Streaming videos isn't something you'll be able to do while driving. However, it's a great option for something that you can do while you're at a hotel or motel.

Streaming services usually run a little over ten dollars a month. However, look for companion deals with various cellular phone services and other companies. You can run them on a variety of devices from laptops and tablets to smartphones.

Hobbies

You will have downtime while you are waiting for load gigs or the actual freight and you can't spend all of it staring at your smartphone waiting for work.

Consider bringing along some type of activity or hobby. While they are going to be welcome on overnights and in motel and hotel rooms, you may be able to enjoy things such as reading and maybe even crafts while you have downtime. You can always bring books or read e-books on your device.

Some drivers (male and female) take up knitting or other sewing projects. Just don't choose something that you can't put down quickly when it's time for your next gig. For example, doing jigsaw puzzles in the cab is probably not the best hobby to have.

Parking

It's not one of the things that come to mind at first, but that doesn't make it any less important.

You'll need to have a place to park your trailer while not on the road. Check to make sure there are no local zoning regulations if you plan to keep it at home.

Some cities might require you to keep the trailer on a special concrete pad in your backyard, while some cities may not allow the trailer to be stored on the premises whatsoever.

If you need to find a location to store your trailer during downtime, look for one that is safe and secure. You don't want to pull up ready for a load and find your trailer has been vandalized, broken, or stolen. Also, make sure to budget this into your main budget.

On the road, you will need to find places to park your truck and trailer overnight.

Many hotels and motels, especially on highway trucking lanes, offer locations near lodging to park. Often, they are well-lit and secure but make sure to investigate for yourself before you leave your load overnight.

Always check that your load is secure, properly locked, and covered. Do not assume that your load will be safe "for a few" hours in a vacant lot or on the side of the road. Check with a location before leaving to make sure it isn't damaged, ticketed, or towed.

Loneliness

While most of your runs will most likely just be day runs, there may be times when you find yourself on the road for extended amounts of time. To some, driving is a solitary, almost meditative act, but for others, it's a new unusual experience and might not be something you are used to.

With a smartphone, it's easy to reach out and talk to people. But, sometimes, it's not about that. Many people just don't like being surrounded by other people, but it doesn't mean they wouldn't mind some companionship in the cab.

So, you could always go old school and bring your pet, although, realize that this does create other responsibilities, but you know your pet better than anyone else.

If you do bring a pet with you, make sure you bring necessary items such as a food and water bowl, a leash, cleaning supplies for when they do their business, toys, and possibly a pet crate.

If driving takes you away from family, have something special planned with them for when you return.

Solitude can also be a time of introspection. It doesn't have to be deep, and you should be paying attention to your driving, but you can use this time to plan jobs and think over projects.

And you may find that you actually don't enjoy hotshotting alone and want a partner. You could always hire an assistant if things are going well or bring in your spouse. They might even be interested in coming along on the business with you and you could possibly expand to two trucks if you really wanted to. The family that hotshots together stays together!

Driving at Night

Driving at night is a different experience. A hotshotter not only needs to worry about safety on the road and what they can see, but they also have to be concerned about tiredness and fatigue behind the wheel.

Use your high beams at night so you can get a full view of the road, but make sure not to blind other drivers. Turn them off within 500 feet of a vehicle coming towards you or when you're right behind another vehicle. And don't look directly into the lights of oncoming vehicles or it could cause temporary blindness or loss of a clear view.

Make sure to keep your windshield clean and your windshield wiper blades kept up to par. Dirt, dust, and water can block your view, cause light distortions, or create reflections that make driving dangerous.

Distracted driving is always something to not do, and it is illegal in most states, but at night, it can be even more deadly. In low light, your eyes may not respond or react as quickly as you look around. Plus, you need more time to react in the dark, and looking up from the phone, radio, or paperwork will lessen this time.

At the same time, you need to be aware of your physical condition. If you are feeling fatigued, or becoming groggy, or finding that you are missing exits or not reacting quickly, you need to pull over and rest.

You can also keep your cab a bit cooler and it will help, but only so much. Watching your diet will also help. Heavy, carb-filled food will make you sleepy. Be careful of drinking energy or sugar drinks. You will feel very awake for a while, but there will be a crash afterwards, which can be dangerous. The same can happen with coffee.

Make sure you get proper rest at night, especially if you have early runs or a long day. Put away phones and computers well before bedtime so your body has a chance to wind down before you go to sleep.

Etiquette

While on the road, there are certain ways that truckers of all sizes interact with each other.

- Always say thank you, whether verbally or non verbally. A wave or a flash of your lights will let them know your appreciation.
- Flash your headlights to let another trucker know they are clear when passing.
- Be aware of other trucks trying to merge from ramps or getting up to speed. Drivers in cars often don't understand the dangers or difficulties of driving with a trailer, so you may need to be the one who helps out or intervenes.
- When driving next to cars, be aware that they may not understand how a trailer works or the dangers

of a rig setup. Be careful and ready in case something happens because the car driver may not know what to do if your trailer sways or other things occur.

Safety

Exercising basic caution will usually be enough but there are certain situations you may find yourself in where you should be a bit more wary.

- Never pick up hitchhikers or riders you don't know. Not only is it a danger, but it might actually invalidate parts of your commercial insurance policy if anything happens to you or the truck. Also, check policy provisions before allowing known riders like family in the cab.
- Always park your truck and trailer in well-lit and secure areas. Avoid leaving it on the side of the road or where it can be a target for theft or vandalism.
- Always wear your seat belt. Never text and drive and always use a hands-free kit or headset for phone calls.
- If you are new to driving a truck of the size you purchased, consider a safety or skills course to become familiar with it.
- Check your mirrors often. Always stay aware while driving. If you are not experienced hauling a trailer, this can be a real problem. Consider practicing your driving, backing up, and other maneuvers in a large parking lot or other location.
- Always be aware of weather and potential shifts. Consider this while prepping your load.
- Always be aware of the cushion of space around your vehicle.

Guns and Trucking

Some truckers choose to carry guns with them in the cab in order to protect themselves. While it is a personal choice, make sure you follow all the laws of your individual state. There is no federal law prohibiting you from keeping a weapon in your truck.

If you choose to carry a gun, you may need proper permits for carried or concealed weapons. Be aware that your permit may not be valid in other states, so if you cross state lines, you may need to reconsider bringing it.

If you do have a weapon, make sure to transport it safely. Also, consider taking a gun safety course, which actually may be required in order to get your permit.

Other options for safety include less lethal measures. Many truckers will carry a Taser (which is regulated in some states), pepper spray, a knife, or a baseball bat.

Gambling

With the growth of Indian Casinos and legalized gambling across the country, gambling issues aren't just for drivers that travel to Las Vegas or Atlantic City anymore.

Casinos go out of their way to appeal to truckers with not just gambling but food, easy and safe parking, and other amenities. For most, it is a refuge from the road for a few hours of fun, but for some with gambling problems, it's a major issue.

Addicted gamblers have an inability to accept the reality of their situation and feel most in control when they are gambling. Of special problem for female addicted gamblers are slot machines, which have been shown to provide women a sense of control due to it just being them and the machine. This illusion leads them to gamble more thinking they're in charge of their fate when in reality, the machine is taking control from them.

Because of the length of time away from home and easy access to casinos, it's a real problem for truckers of all types. Often, it savagely attacks younger drivers who often haven't established themselves or dealt with addictive issues.

If gambling is a problem for you, please seek help and assistance. Many truck stops offer support groups, not just for alcohol and drugs but for gambling as well.

Prostitution

In the parlay of long haul truckers, prostitutes are often called "lot lizards" or other derogatory names. It can be a real problem at truck stops and other locations where truckers congregate. In the days of the CB heavy trucking use, prostitutes would have their own handles and contact drivers over the radio to up appointments.

Aside from any moral issues about the profession, using the services of a prostitute can put you in several areas of danger. First of all, from a health concern, you are putting your self at risk of disease. There is also a safety concern due to the fact that many prostitutes work in conjunction with thieves and will roll a driver, stealing money, belongings, and even their truck and load.

Also, if you are arrested soliciting a prostitute, you will be fined, face jail time, and be at the risk of losing your truck and business.

Drugs

Even though truckers are required to take a DOT drug test, there is a large problem with drug use in the industry. Often, drivers will use amphetamines or other drugs to keep themselves moving and awake. Some drivers use other drugs for performance or due to personal preference.

If you have an accident, even if you were not under the influence at the time, you may be required to submit to a drug test. If you fail, you risk losing your license, documentation, and possibly your business.

Smoking

Aside from a lack of exercise, sleep, and healthy food, there is one last problem that is a large issue with truck drivers as relating to health and long haul drivers—smoking.

Smoking has long been a part of truck driving. In the old days, it was a way to pass the time and stay awake. Not only for the activity itself, but drivers would keep cigarettes in their hands so the heat when it burned down would keep them awake as it burned their knuckles. The stress of being a driver has also been attributed to high-smoking rates.

Smoking in a closed area like a truck cab also leads to a savage double dose of smoke. Not only are drivers taking in the harmful smoke first hand, but it also lingers in the cab and they continue breathing it like a fish trapped in a smoke-filled bowl.

As the world moved away from smoking, the trucking industry was slow to follow.
Already at risk for disease because of other factors, studies have shown that truck drivers have a fifty percent higher rate of diabetes and nearly 90 percent of drivers show signs of hypertension or pre-hypertension.

The smoking of cigarettes is responsible for nearly a half million deaths every year. That breaks down to one in five deaths being attributed to smoking. Worldwide, it causes 6 million deaths every year.

Here are some ways to help you break the habit:

- Clear out your home and truck from anything related to cigarettes. Matches, ashtrays, lighters, and paraphernalia. Even stuff with logos on it. Clean and detail your truck cab to remove and smell nicotine or related stains.
- Change your habits, because many times, it relates directly to cigarette use.
- Be patient. It's not going to be easy. But if you can make it past the first week, your chances of succeeding are increased exponentially.
- Depending on your usage, consider the patch or nicotine gum. However, realize that you are still getting the bad effects on your body, albeit in a lower amount. This is good if you have a lifetime addiction, or it's more physical than habitual.
- Eat healthier while quitting. A lot of people turn to food to deal with cravings, but unfortunately, they usually turn to sugar or processed food to make them "feel better" and end up gaining a large amount of weight. If you use snacks, eat healthy ones like fruits and vegetables. Try raisins because some studies have shown that nutrients in raisins actually counteract the craving for nicotine.
- Drink large amounts of water. This will help flush out the toxins that are trapped in your body. It can take weeks to flush these out and you may be coughing up after that. Water will help speed up this process and help you feel better as well.
- Tell people, but tell the right people. Tell your best friends and family because these are the people who will be the most supportive. Try to refrain from announcing your decision on social media until it's successful. When you use an online platform, you risk failing publicly and people can be less than supportive. Your friends and family will be your true

support because they want to see you succeed. Then maybe, when you hit the six-month mark, start telling everyone online.

Chapter 6 - What to Do When the Unexpected Happens on the Road

Roadside Assistance

There are a number of companies that will provide roadside assistance to you as a truck driver. If you have purchased a new truck, often, it will come with a roadside assistance package.

Also, check your insurance policy. You may have lined items that include truck and trailer towing, rental reimbursement, and other coverage. Be sure to ask your insurance agent about this.

Breakdowns

First and foremost, do your best to steer your truck and trailer off the main road. If you can find a solid shoulder, use it, but don't run your truck and trailer into soft dirt or sand. It will only cause more damage. If possible, try to get onto a runaway lane or other place that is stable and out of the way.

Investigate the problem. If it is something you can fix without further assistance, do so as quickly and carefully as possible. Before starting any sort of repair, make sure to set out any required road triangles, flares, or other materials to signify the danger of a vehicle off the road.

Make sure that any work you are doing does not place you in danger of oncoming traffic.

If the work required is beyond what you can fix, call for assistance. If you have a roadside assistance plan (which I highly recommend), contact them and arrange for assistance. Depending on your location, you may be waiting a while, so, make yourself comfortable. Be sure to stay hydrated, especially if you have broken down in a remote location or one with hot temperatures.

Stay in your vehicle. You are safer in your vehicle than sitting on the side of the road or examining your truck.

If this is causing a delay in your delivery, then arrange for a pickup from another driver or contact your client.

Accidents

Truck driving has consistently topped the list of some of the deadliest occupations in the United States, but it's not the inherent danger of the job, it's the accidents on the road. In 2015, over 761 truck drivers were killed on the road. Over the previous five years, trucker fatalities rose steadily by 11 percent.

Experts have said that this increase has been due to the need for rapid delivery coming from the rise of online shopping and next day delivery. Too often, drivers are urged- by companies or themselves- to go after the reward of finishing enough deliveries and lose sight of safety concerns.

Never leave the scene of an accident. If there is significant damage, call for a police officer to file a report for insurance.

Always check to make sure the freight has not been damaged no matter how small or insignificant the accident is. Check all tie-downs and straps and see that it is secure.

If there is damage to the freight, immediately contact your insurance company. Also, contact the client, explain the situation, and ask how they would like to proceed.

If you are injured, seek medical attention. Make sure you have your emergency contact information on you.

Damaged or Lost Loads

If your load becomes damaged or shifts, pull over immediately. Check for slippage of ropes, straps, or chains. If you are unable to fix the load, call for assistance. Never drive a trailer where the freight is not properly strapped into place.

Contact your client about the damage or issues. Be straightforward and honest, but calm and succinct. Inquire how the client would like to proceed. They may want the load returned to its point of origin or instruct you to continue the delivery.

If your load falls from the trailer and onto the roadway, stop immediately. Depending on the situation, you may require not only law enforcement assistance in cleaning up the freight, but you may be required to file a police report. Most likely, insurance companies will want the report for any potential investigations. Again, contact your client and apprise them of the situation.

What about the Freight?

You are bonded to deliver the freight to its destination. It is your responsibility; if your truck breaks down, you need to make arrangements to have your trailer picked up by someone and delivered to its destination.

If you can't call a friend, coworker, or fellow hotshotter who owes you a favor, then you might even have to get on the boards and hire someone else and take a hit.

If you absolutely have to leave the freight on the side of the road for any amount of time, make sure it is secure and tarped if possible.

Trailer Sway and Fishtails

Trailer sway can be set off by a large wind gust, icy roads, sudden braking, or even the passing of a large vehicle like an 18-wheeler. If you have incorrect tire pressure in your trailer tires, this can make a bad situation much worse.

Even before you start driving, there are things you can do to lower the possibility of swaying:

- Make sure your tires are properly inflated.
- Always be aware and driving defensively. Be ready for the unexpected.
- Use lower gears going uphill. On the way down, be gentle in using brakes.
- Consider anti-sway devices and hitches.
- Take potential sway-inducing situations such as icy roads, bridges, and wind gusts very carefully.

If sway happens, do not slam on your brakes or you will begin to fishtail or possibly jackknife if you lose directional control. Reduce your speed gradually and apply the trailer brakes, which will help the situation.

As soon as possible, pull over to a safe place on the side of the road and examine the trailer to make sure it was the wind or an environmental issue and not because the trailer is damaged. It is also possible something may have come loose or have been damaged in the incident.

Natural Disasters

You may never have to worry about this, but there are drivers who get caught in earthquakes, tornadoes, fires, and even in riots.

The first rule is your life is more valuable than your truck. Even your client would agree that the part you were transporting can be replaced, while your life cannot.

So, if you find yourself in danger, abandon your truck and find safety. There may be times when you can safely lock up your truck and return, while other times will be a race for your life. We have all seen the horrible video of floods or earthquakes where drivers only have moments before their vehicle is washed away or crushed under a falling overpass.

Find safety and do not leave until you know it is safe or are told that it is. Contact your friends and family immediately to let them know you are safe. Then contact your insurance company and your client to update them on the situation.

Again, your life and safety are of the utmost importance.

Theft

Prevention will ward off most average thieves. Make sure the cargo is secure and locked if possible. Make sure the doors are locked as well as any lockboxes.

For some reason, some people are against using tarps, but if you use them, they can be a great way to seal in cargo and lessen the temptation for people to mess with it. Having to look under a well-strapped tarp is usually a bit more effort than most common thieves or criminals are willing to give.

If you do find that you have been robbed, contact the police and get a full report. Contact your insurance company. If the theft impacted your client's cargo, contact them and give them a brief assessment of the situation and confirm that they want to continue the delivery or make other plans.

In your contracts for employment, it is either as an independent contract or through websites that will have clauses on theft liability. Consult them to know where you stand.

Armed Robbery

Armed robbery has always been a problem for truckers. When they are away from their cab getting fuel or even at a rest stop, they are tired, often a bit distracted, and not paying attention to their surroundings. This is when attacks are most likely to occur. The news is littered with stories of truck drivers being held up at gun or knife point for the money they have on them, their truck, or their freight.

Hijacking and cargo theft are real issues as well. According to federal statistics in 2016, over 600 trucks were stolen with over 700 trailers, which is a steady increase over previous years. It's estimated that theft and robbery accounted for losses of over $170 million dollars in the span of a year.

According to statistics, Los Angeles is the number one location for cargo theft with other high crime areas including the New York metro area and the south, primarily Texas, Oklahoma, and Northern Louisiana.

In the trucking industry, there is a saying "Cargo at rest, is cargo at risk." Always be aware of your surroundings and that of your rig and trailer. Park in well-lit areas even if you are only going to be gone for a few minutes. Always be aware of your surroundings and who you are interacting with. Also, never allow someone else to handle or transport your cargo unless you know who they are.

If you are highly concerned or in an area that has a high level of robbery or theft, consider a tracking device in your truck and trailer as well as an alarm and recovery system for your vehicle.

Health Issues or Emergencies

Make sure that your health insurance is valid in the areas you are traveling to. If for some reason your haul takes you across the border to a foreign country, make sure that your health insurance is valid there. You might need to purchase a temporary rider which can be purchased online for a few dollars a day.

Keep open communication with people so they know who you are dealing with and where you are traveling to.

Fatigue

There was a time when truckers wore their exhaustion as a badge of honor. They would gather at the truck stop, swigging coffee and caffeine pills, and laugh about how long it had been since they slept.

Fast forward to today, public awareness, legislation, and a change in self-awareness has changed all of that.

You need to get enough rest, and if you are tired, pull over. Do not use supplements. Never falsify your logbook if you are working more than allowable hours.

You are risking your life and the lives of others. Pull over and rest. No load is worth a crash.

DUI

Never consume alcohol before operating any vehicle, let alone your work vehicle. If you get pulled over, arrested, and charged with driving under the influence, you are in danger of not only losing your license, but your business, your truck, and possibly your freedom. If you have employees, you need to have the same policy with them. This is a serious matter.

If you or one of your employees is arrested for DUI- and this includes not only medical and recreational marijuana but over-the-counter drugs and painkillers as well, be sure to contact an attorney immediately. This is one of the most serious things that can happen to you as an owner-operator and you are at risk of losing everything. Consult with your attorney about how to progress.

Arrest

There are many things that could lead to your arrest, and you may not even know it's coming. You may have a suspended license you aren't aware of or outstanding tickets that have led to a bench warrant. You may have even been in the wrong place at the wrong time and gotten into an altercation and ended up in the back of a police car. Or you may not have even done anything and are a victim unjustly accused.

None of that matters to your client. It's one thing if you are in a dangerous situation and you need to protect yourself. Most clients aren't going to accept "I'm in jail" as an excuse for not getting their load delivered. It's not their fault, so that leaves one last responsible person…you.

Make sure to find a way to contact someone to deal with your truck and load as soon as possible. You may be calling your attorney or your family, but make sure someone can deal with that loaded trailer and finish the job.

Your truck also might be impounded as well as your trailer. Just because you are behind bars, even temporarily or unjustly, your business doesn't stop.

Chapter 7 - Common Mistakes Truck Drivers Make That Can Run Them Out of Business

Not Following Government Regulations

Many drivers just starting out don't think that regulations are important or think they can get by for a while until their business is large enough. However, this can get you into trouble from day one. You need to keep a record of hours of service, logbooks, and other information. It may seem like a lot of paperwork but it will keep you legal and also help when it comes time for accounting, taxes, and possible payroll.

When in doubt, ask. Contact the local department and talk with someone or arrange for a time to visit your local office. Ignorance is not a valid excuse when it comes to the government.

Hiring the Wrong Staff

When a business is just starting out, money is tough and help is even tighter. You may find that you need assistance in maintenance or accounting or that your business has grown enough that you want to hire more drivers.

Make sure you interview and check out any potential employees. Check on their background and references. You don't want to hire someone who is going to run your business into the ground or possibly steal from you.

Also, treat them well and with respect. There is a large shortage of drivers in the industry and always jobs for drivers. You don't want to have an issue with an employee and then quit and leave your load on the side of the road.

Not Understanding or Accounting For Taxes

All too often, new businesses run up against local, state, and federal tax issues because they didn't take the time to understand the law. Make sure you not only keep good records and set aside funds to pay taxes, but hire a reputable accountant with experience in the trucking industry to make sure everything is filed properly and correctly.

Maintenance

Brand new truck, brand new trailer, and gear... what could go wrong?

Plenty of things that's what.

Maintenance is very important. If you don't keep up on the scheduled maintenance, cleaning, and upkeep, your entire business could suffer. It starts with something as simple as a faulty strap that could lead to a load shifting and being damaged. Or it could be something bigger like a blown engine or axle issues.

It is important to keep up on maintenance and keep logs of all the work that's been done.

Cash Flow

Sometimes, it can up to 60 days before you get paid on your hauls. However, you still need to pay bills, so it's possible that you could find yourself doing well on paper, but with no money to pay your bills. Some owners paint themselves into a corner and have no cash flow. It can kill a business.

Health

If a driver goes down for a few days or weeks due to health or injury, their ability to make money stops. If you are the owner-operator, this destroys your business.

This makes it incredibly important to take care of yourself. Get enough rest, exercise, and get regular checkups. If you are on medication, make sure you follow the directions. If you injure yourself, make sure to take the time and proper steps to heal or else you may find yourself laid up with a much worse injury.

Not Accounting for Downtimes

There will be times, especially in the early days of your hotshotting business, where you may not be able to get any gigs, or not enough to show a profit. Times will change, but like any business, there can be some ups and there can be some downs. The industry can be seasonal with slow times later in the year.

Some owner-operators budget themselves so tightly that the loss of income for only a few days could be enough to destroy their entire business. Be careful of this. Don't keep too much overhead or bills that if you lose cash liquidity, you will incur fees or something even worse.

Always expect the unexpected. Be thankful when you get work, but always be hustling for the next job.

Under budgeting

Not unique to hotshot trucking, many new small businesses neglect to properly budget. They don't account for issues that are going to pop up or just generally don't understand what they are going to have to lay out.
Driving a hotshot truck is no different. There will be unforeseen maintenance fees due to wear and tear, load

issues, trailer damage, and harm from potholes, highways, and other unforeseen factors.

The reality is that by not being prepared, you could find damage or problems you can't pay for and this can keep you off the road, and possibly be the downfall of the business.

Make sure to add in a contingency amount into your operating budget that varies from 10-20 percent.

The Ever-Rising Cost of Fuel

Fuel is going to be one of the biggest expenses to your business, and every day, it seems to be rising higher and higher. Make sure to allow for a fuel budget (and a potential contingency). The overrun alone, if you don't prepare for it, can sink your company.

Look for reward point programs, bulk purchases, and other ways to squeeze every penny out of your tank. Also, while on the road, look into phone apps that will help you find the lowest available prices in your area.

Unrealistic Expectations

While you are now in charge of your own business and the potential appears unlimited, you aren't going to get rich as a hotshotter. If you think that you are going to be able to work a couple days a week and be okay, you are mistaken.

If a new hotshot business owner goes into this with unrealistic expectations thinking this is the road to easy stress, they are doomed to fail unless they turn around this mentality quickly. They need to realize that just like any other business; it requires a massive amount of energy to be successful. Be realistic about your goals as a business and how much money you will be bringing in. Also, be very realistic about profit and loss.

Not keeping good documentation

Not just log books but expenditures, receipts, and statements. When it comes time for taxes, you're going to need to work with your accountant and provide all of the necessary information. Many business owners have found themselves in trouble when they are unable to document their expenses. Or worse, during an audit, you need to be ready as a business. Many companies have incurred large fees and fines for not being able to document their business finances.

There are digital programs and apps that can help you organize and document your receipts. Many simple bookkeeping software programs will also allow you to at least take care of your own receipts, even if someone else handles your main finances.

Not Asking For Help

You are going to need help sometimes. It might be the filing out of documents or applications; you'll definitely need accounting help when it comes to your taxes to make sure they are done correctly. You may just need help with directions sometimes as well.

There will also be times when you need to consult an attorney. It might be basic contracts or it could be an accident or an interstate issue. Some of these things need different skills so know when to turn to an attorney.

Don't be too proud to ask for help. There's nothing wrong with it. It's not a sign of weakness; it's actually a place of strength because you are gathering information which makes you better informed, and therefore, stronger.

Being Inflexible

Flexibility is important as a driver and as a business owner. Never be complacent, thinking you have learned everything. Look into classes and seminars about business, repair, trucking, and anything else that you believe could make you a smarter owner-operator.

Keep up to date on new technology, fuel efficiency, and equipment. Even drivers with decades of experience need to keep up on changes in the transportation industry.

It's also important to make changes to your business based upon customer response. By gathering feedback from your clients, you can make changes to your business that makes you more effective and efficient.

Poor Management

Some drivers love being drivers but hate running a business. They just want to be on the road, feel the thrill of scoring the load and the sense of accomplishment of dropping the freight off at its destination.

However, there is much more to running a hotshot business than the deliveries. A business owner needs to manage the operations and this includes everything aside from just the freight delivery. You need to know everything not just about your operations, but also the entire industry. The more you learn, the more successful you will be.

An owner-operator needs to be able to manage all of these things in order to be successful. Not paying attention is a clear road to failure.

Fraud

In today's world, fraud and identity theft are real issues and can take down a company. If an owner isn't aware, they might lose everything they've worked for.

- Don't ever give out financial information without verifying the person you are giving it to and the exact purpose.
- Keep an eye on accounts and contact bank or credit card companies immediately.
- Be careful of load board scams.
- Always make sure your pin number is not being viewed when in use. Also, learn to look for signs of card skimmers at ATMs and gas pumps.
- Always have documents signed by customers. Use contracts when needed.
- Change all passwords regularly.
- Don't give out a lot of specific facts and workings of your business. Definitely be careful of giving out personal information.
- Follow the old saying- if it's too good to be true, then it probably is.

Discipline and Time Management

Being your own boss carries its own problems and one of those is discipline. You won't have anybody looking over your shoulder making sure you are on track for that next job. No one will make sure you are working as hard as you can or that you provide the best customer service possible.

It's up to you to stay organized and focused. Without a time clock, it is easy to slack off. However, that will quickly catch up with you. Set goals and make sure you follow through on them. Even creating eating schedules and break times can help you on your way to organizational time management.

Personal time is also part of time management. Don't run yourself into the ground thinking about business from the moment you open your eyes in the morning to when your head hits the pillow. Give yourself time to relax and get away from work. Spend time with family and friends and unwind.

You might be surprised that you actually come up with some great ideas for work when you finally get a chance to relax.

Home Life

While it may not be your business that is going under, your home life can suffer from a life on the road and that can lead to more issues with your business.

Although, as a hotshot trucker, you have the option of staying close to home and not going on long road trips. However, that isn't the only stress that can put pressure on your marriage and relationship with your spouse and children. Starting a business is stressful. You are going to have concerns about keeping your business going, and growing your business can cause rifts with your loved ones, even causing you to be short with them and pull away. Because you are so concentrated on building your trucking company, you may not notice you are having domestic problems until it is too late. And if you end up getting divorced, your company (even with an LLC protection) can become a bargaining chip in the proceedings.

Make time for your family and really be there for them. Keep one eye on them and the other glued to load boards or financials. Be present and mindful. They will understand that you need your work time, but you also need to understand that you all need together time as well.

Not Diversifying

If a hotshot trucker decides too early on to only work in a niche or tries to only target certain client demographics, they are limiting themselves and doomed to fail.

The more an owner/operator is open to different types of loads, the more opportunities you have to make money. Also, consider getting certifications that can allow you to work with chemicals, perishable, or hazardous materials.

The more your company brings to the table, the more opportunities you will have to be behind the wheel and making money.

Organization

Your business will involve a lot of paperwork, both literally and digitally. You need to make sure you manage it. A business owner who doesn't stay organized is just preparing for failure.

It can also play into the way you perform your job on the road. If you aren't organized and prompt, you will lose jobs and gain a bad reputation. Have your information, location, and client contact information organized.

It's Just Not Right for Them

Hotshot trucking is an awesome business. It has incredible perks and freedoms and opportunities to make money. But that doesn't mean it's for everyone.

A new owner operator may find that they have made a mistake. That it turns out they don't enjoy the business or driving. They hate traffic, they get stressed out when they're behind the wheel, or they can't handle clients and load boards. The constant scrambling for their next gig is giving them anxiety.

So they need to make a choice. Is this job something they will learn to like? Or should they cut their losses and close up shop?
If they keep with it, they risk running the business into the ground and losing all of their initial investment and maybe more. Then you walk away with absolutely nothing.

Many people do things that they don't want to do for a living. It's not about enjoying it; it's about bringing home a paycheck and putting food on the table. However, you can't have that type of attitude with a small business. An owner who is just going through the motions and actually hates what they do isn't going to be successful. They are going to run the company into the ground. You can't raise a beautiful flower garden if you are allergic to flowers and hate them.

So, that owner might need to make the difficult decision to close up. Sell off their gear, truck, and equipment and try something else. Or they might partner with a driver and have them do the driving and they'll handle the office work and business side of operations.

Appendix: HotShot Trucking Glossary

- Agricultural exemption - an exemption from route and rate regulation in a motor carriage when the carrier is hauling basically raw/unprocessed agricultural products.
- Auto carrier - a trailer specially designed to carry automobiles
- Bill of sale - a document given by a seller to the buyer to show the transfer of title of a property.
- Broker - an agent who negotiates freight contract and agreements
- Contract carrier - a for-hire driver who subcontracts with a trucking company or other business.
- Deadhead - driving with an empty trailer when you are on duty.
- Drive Axle - an axle that has powered wheels
- Dually or duallies - trucks with multiple tires in the rear.
- Electronic onboard recorder - A device that records speed, location, and other information.
- ETA - estimated time of arrival
- Factoring Fees - the fees a factoring company or agent charges you
- Flatbed - a trailer without doors or sides. Can usually be loaded or unloaded from any direction.
- For hire - a non-contracted driver who hires out their services to the general public or companies.
- Freight bill - the freight shipment document that gives a description, its weight, amount of charges, and other information.
- Freight Factoring - the use of a third party service to get an advance on an invoice for a small fee.

- Header board - the barrier at the front of a trailer to prevent freight from moving forward. Can also be called a bulkhead.
- Landing Gear - on some trailers, legs that are cranked or moved into place so the trailer is not lying on the ground when unattached.
- Load Boards - the online services or app where you find your jobs.
- LTL - Less than truckload. Also called partial loads.
- Manifest - a document that has the details on a shipment
- MC Number - motor carrier number
- Non-Divisible - freight that cannot be broken down into a smaller load
- Owner-Operator - an independent driver who owns and operates his own truck.
- Platform body - trailer that has floor but no side or roof.
- Point of origin - the place where the freight is taken from the shipper
- Pusher axle - an unpowered axle, also can be called tag axles.
- Receiver - the person who is receiving a shipment
- Shipper - the person who initiated a shipment.
- Skeletal trailer - a trailer that allows for specific cargo containers to be locked into place.
- Team drivers - two or more drivers who drive the same truck, usually in shifts. Allows them to spend more time on the road.
- Terminal - a dock or shipping location that sends freight in various directions in transport.
- Tractor - another name for a Class Eight semi-truck that hauls a trailer. A hotshot truck is not called a tractor.
- Waybill - a description of the shipment sent with the shipment.

Truck classes:

- One - A light truck, up to 6,000-pound weight limit
- Two - A light truck, 6,001 to 10,000-pound weight limit.
- Three - Medium truck, weight limit 10,001 to 14,000-pound weight limit.
- Four - Medium truck, weight limit 14,001 to 16,000 pounds
- Five - Medium truck, weight limit 16,001 to 19,500 pounds
- Six - Medium truck, weight limit 19,501 to 26,000 pounds
- Seven - Heavy truck, weight limit 26,001 to 33,000 pounds
- Eight - Heavy truck, weight limit over 33,000 pounds
- Nine - Super heavy or special use truck, over 33,000 pounds weight limit

CB Codes

While the use of citizen band radio has decreased due to cellular phones, there are still those who use radios in their trucks. You will also hear words and codes used in conversation that are holdovers from the old days of trucking. You may hear many of these and more from older drivers.

- Copy - understood
- Alligator – a piece of blown tire on the roadway
- Bambi - a deer
- Brake check- a traffic jam which will require you to slow down.
- Come back- a request for a reply
- Double nickel- driving 55
- Eyeball - to view or see something
- Lost Wages - Las Vegas

- Back door - behind someone
- Hot mic - when a CB radio user will not stop talking or has their radio keyed on but not using it.
- 10-1, 10-2 - often used to signify bathroom breaks
- 10-4 - message received
- 10-6 - I'm busy
- 10-20 or 20 - location
- 10-99 - All done, job done

Conclusion

With all this information under your belt, you should feel secure in opening your own hotshot company.

The biggest lesson to take away from all of this information is that there are many ways to do things, but there are a few ground rules you need to follow on the road to success.

Always be attentive and careful. Whether it's the purchase of your truck, getting your loads, or while you are traveling, the more you pay attention, the more successful you will be.

It's okay to seek answers or ask for help. If you don't know something, find the answer.

Look online, re-read this book, or ask someone who has more experience than you. The majority of truck drivers- hotshot and Class 8- are really nice people and happy to share their knowledge.

Be on time, courteous, and organized. By doing this, you will create a reputation for yourself and your business, and happy clients will help it grow.

Be positive and hardworking. Building a business isn't easy, but it can be rewarding. Every day, you will face setbacks as well as experience successes.

As you move forward as a hotshotter, you'll still face troubles but you'll find that as you gain experience, you'll be able to handle them easier and easier and find you have more good experiences than bad.

A positive mental outlook will help and your clients and customers will certainly notice.

Best of luck and I look forward to seeing you out on the road!

Did you enjoy reading this book? If so, please consider leaving a review. Even just a few words would help others decide if the book is right for them.

Best regards and thanks in advance—Colton

www.ingramcontent.com/pod-product-compliance
Lightning Source LLC
Chambersburg PA
CBHW030659220526

45463CB00005B/1841